Grassroots Success!

Preparing Schools and Families for Each Other

Valora Washington
Valorie Johnson
Janet Brown McCracken
for the W.K. Kellogg Readiness Initiatives

W.K. Kellogg Foundation
National Association for the Education of Young Children

ISBN #0-935989-66-8
Library of Congress Catalog Card #94-74603
NAEYC #722

Published by
National Association for the Education of Young Children
1509 Sixteenth Street, N.W.
Washington, DC 20036-1426

Printed in the United States of America.

Acknowledgements

The leadership and support of these people were instrumental to the success of the W.K. Kellogg Readiness Initiatives and this book:

National Association for the Education of Young Children
Barbara Willer, Elizabeth A. Ford, and Melanie White
W.K. Kellogg Foundation
Marvin McKinney and Steven Peffers
Michael VanBuren and Linda Tafolla for their creative contributions

Produced by
Rita Mhley & Associates, Inc.
Donna Kolis, senior graphics designer
Judith Cullen, associate designer

When you know
where you came from,
you know where you're going.

–Frances Brock Starms

About the W.K. Kellogg Foundation

When we build on young children's strengths and reduce factors that might keep them from reaching their potential, we serve not only individuals, but society and its future as well.

W.K. Kellogg, who established the Kellogg Foundation more than 60 years ago, had vivid evidence of this in his own life. Although he eventually became a magnate in the breakfast cereal industry, as a child in Michigan he endured many of the hardships experienced by pioneer families. Three of his brothers and sisters died in childhood, and he barely survived a bout with malaria. Mr. Kellogg's formal schooling was minimal; not until he was 20 did he learn that he was nearsighted, far too late to prevent his teachers from thinking him dimwitted because he couldn't read the chalkboard.

In 1930, he established the W.K. Kellogg Child Welfare Foundation, which was soon reorganized as the W.K. Kellogg Foundation to broaden its focus. His concern and interest in children and youth remain central to the Foundation as it awards grants in the areas of maternal and child health, child care, and early education. The Foundation's mission is "to help people help themselves through the practical application of knowledge and resources to improve their quality of life and that of future generations."

In the 1990s, the Foundation renewed its long-standing emphasis on children and early intervention. The School Readiness Initiative—getting schools and families ready for each other—directly addresses the Foundation's mission and values. Mr. Kellogg, who was a caring and generous visionary, was also practical and pragmatic. He knew that helping individuals help themselves was the key to success.

The School Readiness Initiatives described here exemplify that knowledge in grassroots undertakings across the country. By staying true to Mr. Kellogg's vision, the Foundation believes children are more likely to achieve bright and vibrant futures.

Contents

We begin with a glimpse at the success stories emerging from W.K. Kellogg Foundation School Readiness Initiatives. Many more appear throughout this book. Others remain to be generated—in our communities and yours—as we prepare schools and families for each other.

Foreword

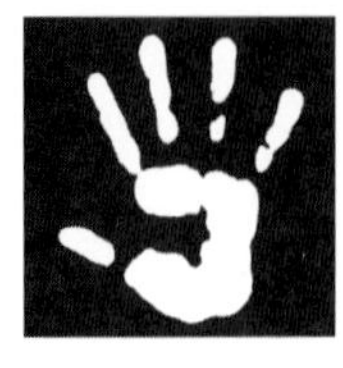

Lori's baby, born 4 weeks premature with respiratory problems, was airlifted to a larger hospital 65 miles away. Lori was frantic, and unable to leave her hospital in Nebraska's Sandhills. The baby's father couldn't risk leaving his new job in another state. Lori's grandmother, 40 miles away, was caring for two other young grandchildren.

Project First Step responded at once. Several times, First Step's director wheeled Lori and her IV into the Initiative's office in the building so Lori could talk by telephone to the nurse caring for her infant. At Lori's release, Project First Step and the baby's hospital arranged transportation, lodging, and meals. Lori stayed with her baby to breastfeed until he was strong enough to come home. Home visits continued until the family joined dad in their new home.

The staff of First Interstate Bank in Houston adopted Success By Six (SBS), a United Way Community Initiative. Bank staff conduct seminars on money management, job preparation, and computers, and provide holiday food baskets.

Other businesses and agencies who support SBS include a television station; the Houston Independent School District; Prudential Insurance Company; the Housing Authority of the City of Houston; Texas Southern University;

Texas Department of Health and Human Services; Houston Police Department; San Jacinto Girl Scouts; Special Supplemental Food Program for Women, Infants and Children (WIC); religious groups; Harlem Globetrotters; the American Red Cross; and the March of Dimes Foundation.

Marjorie Keiser began the Kellogg Preschool Enrichment Program (KPEP) at age 5, the year before kindergarten. Tammy Keiser, her mother, says, "When we first started, she was shy and didn't talk much to people."

A year later, "When she got to school, she had the WANT to learn," reports Fred Keiser, her father.

Now she is 6, in first grade in Tampa, and proud of her school performance. When asked why she liked KPEP, she immediately responds, "It makes me feel good about myself. I like to read books. I like to play. I listen."

According to Marjorie's parents, she spends much of her time at home playing school and restaurant with her older sister and younger brother. Marjorie "wants to be a teacher…to become the next person to run all the schools in the state of Florida. She's already giving her teacher a lot of ideas!" laughs Tammy.

"WOW! It's so ironic. If you're in education you should want to learn and let the learning flow back and forth, where everyone benefits. I learn from the parents, they learn from me, everybody learns from everybody," proclaims enthusiastic kindergarten teacher Merry Hall, in Iron Mountain, Michigan. She is convinced that home visits and families' regular classroom participation are "an A#1 way " to help children succeed in school.

Parent and frequent volunteer Kim Jacobs agrees. "We're just very passionate about it. I'm hooked on this. I hope I can be a little bit of inspiration" to families, children, and educators.

"We're a whole unit working together for our children," they state emphatically.

A 13-year-old male was referred to the Philadelphia Parent Child Center. He had serious behavior problems in and out of school and was failing many classes. After contact with Youth Workers who focus on education, preventive health, positive parenting, self-esteem, and career motivation, his grades moved up to Cs and Bs. His continued progress was so profound that his teacher took him to lunch when he earned his first A.

"It's never too late to start learning," says Bernarda Lopez after completing Avance in Texas' Rio Grande Valley. "I was a mother of 12. As a mother, I was very busy working. Now I have the time to work with my [five] grandchildren and teach them."

Our responsibility is to assure not only that children are eager and able to learn,

but that schools are prepared to promote children's development.

Linking Knowledge With Dreams

A wave of remarkable research results began to capture the national spotlight in the early 1980s. These riveting findings document the importance of high-quality experiences for young children from birth through age five—their most impressionable years. Reams of evidence testify that young children's daily experiences profoundly affect school performance. That impact persists into adulthood.

Policymakers, educators, communities, and families who are aware of these extensive findings realize:

Children are more likely to succeed
—now and in the future—
when schools and families are prepared for each other.

Rhetoric about children's "school readiness" abounds. But is the knowledge about high-quality early experiences backed up with a commitment to make those kinds of experiences happen in our communities and schools?

The W.K. Kellogg Foundation School Readiness Initiatives can answer with a resounding YES! Our 20 initiatives are translating rhetoric into reality. We are improving services to children and families, and integrating systems. Our grassroots efforts are increasing opportunities that lead to success for children, families, schools, and communities.

We invite you—families, educators, public officials, policymakers, advocates—to build on our experiences. Our responsibility is to assure not only that children are eager and able to learn, but that schools are prepared to promote children's development. Let's work together, beginning today, to support bright futures across America by building upon what we already know is effective.

Opportune Moments

When former President George Bush and the nation's governors hammered out their six most important national education goals in 1989, this goal emerged as the first—

Goal One: "By the year 2000, all children will start school ready to learn."

Adoption of Goal One

Three objectives were specified to achieve Goal One:

- all children with disabilities and from less-advantaged families would have access to good quality, appropriate preschool experiences
- every parent would devote time every day to help their preschoolers learn, and they would have access to training and support needed to do that
- children would receive the nutrition and health care needed to arrive at school healthy

Adoption of the voluntary National Education Goals coincided with widespread attention to two decades of research on child development. Numerous studies, many with Head Start, identify specific early experiences that are critical to ensure positive outcomes for children. Their conclusions: Health, nutrition, family and community stability, cultural competence, self-esteem, and the quality of early learning experiences most often predict children's school and life success.

Improvement in even one of these components increases a child's opportunity to succeed in school and in life. Knowledge about these interrelated factors, and the persistence to apply it, is essential. Long-term, integrated changes in family-support systems hold the most promise for life-long success.

Critical components for *children* to achieve their potential

- health
- nutrition
- family and community stability
- cultural competence
- self-esteem
- quality of early learning experiences

Improvement in even one component increases children's opportunities to succeed in school and in life.

All areas of children's development—emotional, language, social, cognitive, and physical—are critical in preparing children and schools for each other. Informed teaching practices and public policies reflect this knowledge.

Health, nutrition, family and community stability, cultural competence, self-esteem, and the quality of early learning experiences predict school and life success.

Goal One triggered these and many other questions for The National Education Goals Panel, a group of elected officials, administrators, and experts:

- What are optimal outcomes for children?
- What are the most effective ways to improve direct services to children and families?
- What are the benefits of integrating pivotal issues such as school reform, Head Start, and other services for children and families?
- What are the most appropriate ways to promote and measure children's progress?

Clearly, not only must children be eager and able to learn, but schools must understand and promote children's development, and families must be able to support their children and schools. This new way of thinking—getting families and schools ready for each other—is the most promising route to children's lifetime success.

Outmoded expectations for children, such as knowing how to count and recite the alphabet, are no longer accepted as valid indicators of "school readiness." All areas of children's development—emotional, language, social, cognitive, and physical—are critical in preparing children and schools for each other. Informed teaching practices and public policies reflect this knowledge.

"Zeal without knowledge is fire without light."

–Thomas Fuller

Professional Practices

Before the National Education Goals began to take shape, early childhood educators were updating professional practices. Standards for high-quality, developmentally appropriate programs for young children were articulated in 1987 by the National Academy of Early Childhood Programs. Established by the National Association for the Education of Young Children (NAEYC), this voluntary accreditation system recognizes early childhood program excellence.

The Academy's multidisciplinary criteria encompass and define *high quality* for all the known critical components of excellent early childhood education:

- interactions among staff and children

- curriculum
- staff-parent interaction
- staff qualifications and development
- administration
- staffing
- physical environment
- health and safety
- nutrition and food service
- evaluation

As the accreditation process gained momentum, kindergarten and primary teachers, as well as elementary school principals, became more aware of teaching methods and learning activities that support positive outcomes for children.

In 1990, the National Association of Elementary School Principals (NAESP) adopted standards that reflect knowledge about how young children learn, and that complement and extend the NAEYC criteria into the elementary years. Both sets of standards are gradually being implemented in early childhood and elementary programs across the country.

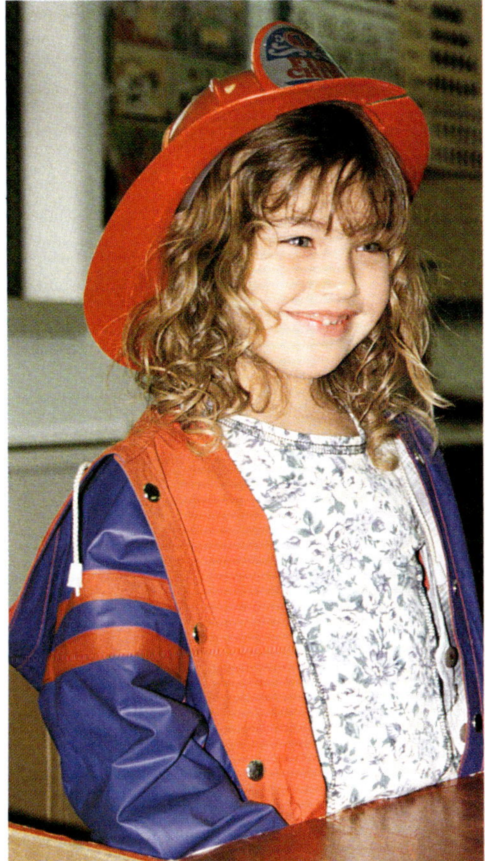

"We could stick with the traditional — children sitting in their seats all day with paper and pencil — but it's not the right thing to do."

–Scott McClure, principal, North and East Elementary Schools, Iron Mountain, Michigan

Schools that are ready for children...

- Welcome all children and families in the community
- Design curriculum content and daily routines that promote children's self-motivated learning: social, emotional, cognitive, and physical
- Offer challenging, hands-on, relevant learning activities that build on what children already know and prepare them to contribute to a democratic society
- Assure that staff are well-prepared to work with the ages and abilities of the children
- Use appropriate methods to assess children's progress and evaluate possible special needs
- Prepare environments that enable children to construct knowledge and understanding through inquiry, play, social interaction, and skill development

*"Knowing is not enough;
we must apply!
Willing is not enough; we must do."*

–Goethe

Public Policy

In contrast to strides made by educators committed to developmentally appropriate practice, public policy progress to address Goal One remains scattered. State and local policies—to integrate service delivery systems and support professional practice—are slow to change. Decisions are often made without consulting people who are most affected. Other efforts languish due to lack of enforcement mechanisms and inadequate resources. Funding for Head Start, even with the conclusive evidence of children's success as adults, allows the program to serve only a fraction of eligible children.

Foundation Support

In 1992, the W.K. Kellogg Foundation stepped in with a School Readiness Initiative to bolster our grassroots voices as we translate national aims into daily action. Children, families, and educators in our 20 communities are striving to prepare children, families, and schools for each other.

Some of our Initiatives strengthen families through calls on new mothers in the hospital, home visits and support groups, and developmentally appropriate experiences for young children. Others screen children's development, offer curriculum guidance, or provide technical assistance on delivery systems. All of us inspire communities to act in ways that are congruent with knowledge about what really counts toward success in young children's lives, today and in the future.

Challenges to Prepare American Children and Schools for Each Other

- Approximately 40% of the nation's children are at risk of school failure. This includes children who are poor, those from minority groups, those with limited command of English, those who live in a single-parent family or with parents who are poorly educated, and those with disabling conditions (National Commission on Children, 1991).
- Child abuse/neglect in 1993 was reported in 15 out of every 1,000 U.S. children (National Committee to Prevent Child Abuse, 1994).
- 10 to 15% of American children have chronic and disabling medical conditions (National Commission on Children, 1993).
- The U.S. ranks lower than 22 other industrialized countries in its infant mortality rate (National Center for Health Statistics, 1993).
- In 1991, Head Start served less than one-third of the eligible children (Stewart & Gabe, 1991).
- Children watch an average of 23 hours of television per week, and will view 200,000 acts of violence by age 18 (American Academy of Pediatrics, 1994).

"Teachers are using more hands-on, more language experience, fewer mimeo sheets. They're more comfortable with manipulatives and skill groups. Children enjoy learning more."

–Joyce Taylor, principal, Thurston Woods Campus, Milwaukee, Wisconsin

- Less than half of preschool children are read to each day (National Commission on Children, 1993).
- "Typically, child care professionals earn only half as much as equally prepared early childhood professionals working within the public school system." In center-based child care, staff turnover rates are nearly 3 times the annual turnover reported by U.S. companies and nearly 5 times the turnover rate reported for public school teachers. Quality of care deteriorates with high turnover rates (Carnegie Corporation of New York, 1994).
- All school readiness tests have error rates in the range of 50% (Shepard & Smith, 1986). Readiness tests cannot predict how children will do in any program (Peck, McCaig, & Sapp, 1988).
- Early childhood programs that stress academic development are not based on current theory or research (Peck, McCaig, & Sapp, 1988). Students in primary grade classes may complete more than 1,000 workbook pages and worksheets in a year (Jachym, Allington, & Broikou, 1989).

We're Making a Difference!

"Companies can recall faulty airplanes or poisonous food, but we can't recall children. They have only one chance to get an education."

—Joan Ganz Cooney

Compelling evidence, gleaned from the diverse achievements of all 20 of our Kellogg School Readiness Initiatives, is presented in this book. All of us who participate—family members, teachers, administrators, board members, community residents, and policymakers—are making a difference.

You can build on our experiences to spark action in your community. Find out what really works. Listen to how lives are changed. Recognize which pitfalls to avoid, and see how to orchestrate effective approaches. Look in these pages for practical recommendations about how to get the most for your money (collaborate!) and how to generate community support.

We urge you to act upon this knowledge, tailor your ideas to local circumstances, and integrate systems. Let's make a lasting difference for our nation's children, families, schools, and communities.

Our Initiatives inspire communities to act in ways that are congruent with knowledge about what really counts toward success in young children's lives.

"No child sits and gets information in this building. We try to read to the children three or four times a day."

–Martha Wheeler-Fair
principal, Frances Starms
Early Childhood Center,
Milwaukee, Wisconsin

Voices of Grassroots Success

The stories described throughout this book come from the participants of the 20 W.K. Kellogg School Readiness Initiatives. Complete descriptions of each Initiative appear in the Appendix.

Avance-Rio Grande Valley, Texas, offers bilingual education for families and their children from birth through age 4. Other components include home visits, family literacy, and transportation.

Be-Four School Project, Charlevoix, Michigan, makes home visits and collaborates with services for children ages 3 and 4.

Creating Collaborative Frameworks for "School Readiness" is working in Colorado, Ohio, and South Carolina to establish integrated, comprehensive state service systems for families with young children.

Delta West Community-Based Project, Little Rock, Arkansas, makes home visits and coordinates services for children up to age 3 who have special needs.

Early Education Services for Parents, Infants, and Preschoolers in rural Allegan County, Michigan, implements home-based education, Even Start in seven school districts, play groups for children ages 3 and 4, and parent support/education groups.

Effective Parent Training and Education Program, Bernalillo, New Mexico, smoothes the transition of 3-year-olds with developmental disabilities from early intervention into Head Start by conducting culturally appropriate parent education and professional development.

Kellogg Preschool Enrichment Program (KPEP), in 3 Florida cities offers home-based parent education and group activities for parents and their children from ages 3 through 5.

Milwaukee Early Schooling Initiative, Milwaukee, Wisconsin, implements integrated early childhood education for children ages 3 through 8; provides family-centered linkages among families, schools, and the community; and enhances professional development for teachers.

My Parent(s) and Me, Battle Creek, Michigan, supports appropriate parenting and teaching skills and connects elementary school parents with community agencies.

Outdoor Learning Center, Battle Creek, Michigan, operates an intriguing outdoor learning area for parents and preschoolers in an elementary school.

Pittsburg Pre-School Coordinating Council Co-op Project (PSCC), Pittsburg, California, increases access to community resources for families with young children.

Project Educational Impact (PEI), Alpena, Michigan, holds monthly dinner meetings in their elementary schools and offers home visits and Parent Mentors to families with children ages birth to 5.

Project First Step, Broken Bow, Nebraska, visits families beginning at the birth of a new baby and acts as an advocate for families with young children.

Promoting Realistic Educator-Parent Awareness for Relevant Education (P.R.E.P.A.R.E.), Iron Mountain, Michigan, assists families, teachers, and administrators in three elementary schools to form community-based programs and supports home visits through 2nd grade.

Pumsey Circuit Breaker, Hillsdale, Michigan, hosts family events to ease the transition into kindergarten; children from kindergarten through 5th grade participate in a self-esteem program.

Quality Transition Program, Battle Creek, Michigan, offers parent support and preschool programs that encourage learning through play.

Smart Start, Battle Creek, Michigan, provides home visits, parenting and nutrition classes, a toy lending library, and resource center in an elementary school for families with children from birth through age 8.

The Staying Ahead Project, Philadelphia, Pennsylvania, encourages youth from 10 to 14 in the areas of health, parenting skills, self-esteem, and career motivation.

Student Readiness Program, Battle Creek, Michigan, involves preschool children and their families in an integrated play area in an elementary school.

Success By Six (SBS), Houston, Texas, supports mothers and children from before birth until age 6 through prenatal care, parent education, and other coordinated services.

Children are influenced by whatever affects their families, so strong families are the starting point.

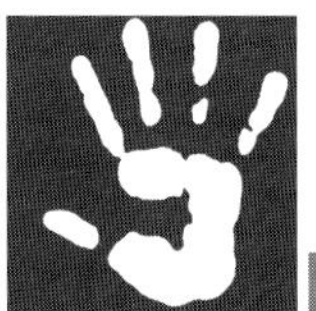

Building Partnerships With Families

"I want to give my children opportunities, to open up the world for them, so they can be the best person they can be."

–Stan Gearhart, parent,
Iron Mountain, Michigan

You are probably eager to see how your state or community could adapt the nuts and bolts of our Kellogg Initiatives. Latching on to bits and pieces is not enough. If you want children and families to succeed, you must craft comprehensive, integrated efforts.

Eight core strategies enable us to successfully prepare children and schools for each other. These strategies are the cement—the stones, water, lime, and clay—upon which your area can integrate its resources. We focus on family-oriented strategies in this chapter, and community components in Chapter 3.

Successful Efforts...

- *Strengthen families*
- *Assure community inclusiveness*
- *Promote cultural competence*
- *Build on community assets*
- *Work for results*
- *Look for partners*
- *Tell everybody*
- *Create a bigger dream*

As you begin to think about how to tailor these strategies to your community, keep in mind all factors that impinge on children's success—health, nutrition, family and community stability, cultural competence, self-esteem, and the quality of early learning experiences. Children are influenced by whatever affects their families, so strong families are the starting point.

Strengthen Families

Families have a profound impact on each child's success. Children learn how to act, how to treat others, even how to learn—primarily at home. When families take an active role in their children's learning, children are far more likely to do well in school and later in life. How do we capitalize on what we know, and work together to build strong families? Many of us focus on children's first teachers—their families—and their relationships at home and school.

"I learned how to be patient and calmly discipline. I explain things to children. I learned about good nutrition for my children, and how to economize."

–Leticia Hernandez, Avance participant

Formal learning commands attention in our society. Important life skills, such as parenting and nutrition, typically receive far less emphasis than traditional school subjects. Families may have been led to believe that teaching means instruction, even of infants. In fact, everyday reading together, eating healthy food, talking about what's happening, and getting along together are among the things that matter the most.

Family-centered early childhood education is one goal set by the Milwaukee Early Schooling Initiative. Two new public schools that enroll young children opened comfortable family resource centers where families discuss topics such as child development, parenting, and community issues. "Parents, kids, young adults—tie them all together," recommends one of our participants. "You can't think or work in a vacuum."

Families Are Children's First Teachers

Lifelong learning begins before birth. Children's development is affected by their parents' health and nutrition. Infants, toddlers, and preschoolers learn the family's language. They "follow the leader" in how they treat people and express feelings. Healthy children gain physical skills as their bodies mature. These everyday learning experiences are key to children's life success.

Strengthen Families

- ***Families are children's first teachers.***
- ***Children live in diverse families.***
- ***All families have strengths.***
- ***Families rely on support networks.***

Children learn how to act, how to treat others, even how to learn—primarily at home. When families take an active role in their children's learning, children are far more likely to do well in school and later in life.

"The important thing is not so much that every child should be taught, as that every child should be given the wish to learn."

–John Lubbock

Families and staff gather in the family resource center to listen as Frances Brock Starms reads her poetry about the long-lasting impact of children's early experiences. She frequently stops by this Milwaukee public school, which was named in her honor.

Children Live in Diverse Families

Every family, every child is unique. "One size fits all" doesn't apply when preparing schools and children for success. "If we go into a family's home, and they have no food, we don't even go into the 'Parents As Teachers' plan," notes Carole Birch with Early Education Services.

"We start where the family is, and that varies," adds Sue Smith Aiken.

In many of our Initiatives, school preparation involves helping a family put food on the table, learn to read, obtain health care, arrange transportation, locate employment, or find housing. The Pittsburg Pre-School Coordinating Council (PSCC) helped one mother find housing and eventually hired her. From there, she went on to attend college.

Families who feel comfortable with their child care providers and children's teachers are more likely to get involved in their children's formal education. "All educators say, 'Our door is always open,' but sometimes you have to do more than talk," observes Johanna Ostwald with P.R.E.P.A.R.E.

What are we doing to ensure that family diversity is appreciated?

Kindergarten teacher Tom Brzezinski knows that children's classroom experiences are heightened by responding to each family's characteristics.

"I am blessed by having a teacher who loves having parents in the room. It changed my whole concept of my role in my child's education. We have a sense of unity...let's do what's best for everyone."

–Kim Jacobs, parent, Iron Mountain, Michigan

Orientations for incoming kindergartners often take on a new twist. Project Educational Impact invites families to evening dinner meetings in school cafeterias. Parents see what kind of meals children eat, and children see their new surroundings in reassuring company. "When the project first started, it was very quiet. Now, you hear, 'Hey, I saved you some seats,'" notes Hinks Elementary School Principal Roger Witherbee. "It's really helped improve lunch room behavior at the beginning of the school year," he adds.

Classroom experiences are also heightened by responding to each family's characteristics. One mother confided to P.R.E.P.A.R.E. kindergarten teacher Tom Brzezinski that her daughter was unhappy at home and rarely shared school information. Brzezinski invited the mother, who has a hearing impairment, to help out with classroom activities. "This little girl witnessed how effective her mother was," Brzezinski recalls. "I think she has a better self-image because of seeing her mom's interaction with other students and her important role in the class."

Sometimes, it's the simple things that count. At Lincoln Elementary School's Smart Start, the Parent's Room has a diaper changing table.

Responding to Families in Diverse Communities on the Texas-Mexico Border

For 21 years, Avance successfully served families in metropolitan areas. The Kellogg Initiatives made it possible for similar programs to be replicated with low-income families in three distinct communities: McAllen, a small city; Linda Vista, a rural colonia with families living in extreme poverty, and La Casita, an established agricultural community.

In the first year, program adjustments included offering all activities in Spanish and English. In rural areas especially, staff found that children with developmental delays were less likely to be referred to appropriate services. Referral networks were developed with early intervention programs, schools, and social services to ease children's transition into school. Avance collaborates with Head Start and elementary schools on transportation, information exchanges, and use of facilities for special events.

Toymaking and parenting classes enable parents to see themselves as their children's teachers who develop children's learning skills. "The children and the parents blossomed," reports Raquel Oliva. She also notes that "although these families live in extreme poverty, sometimes lacking food, living in dilapidated housing without running water, where the kitchen is outdoors and the bathroom is an outdoor privy, we have found that they are extremely optimistic about the future. They have a hope for a better life for their children and they want to learn how they can ensure that success."

Every family has strengths and needs. Our Initiatives find that some family characteristics may be viewed as weaknesses when perceived through the lens of another cultural background. Many of these characteristics are actually strengths. We are learning to capitalize on these strengths rather than limit ourselves to overcoming barriers.

All Families Have Strengths

Mauck Elementary School is situated in a rural community where families have long memories. Instead of seeing negative attitudes about the school district as a hurdle, the Pumsey Circuit Breaker recognized strength and opportunity. "If the kids are happy with school, and their parents are happy with the school, then eventually—and it will take years—that positive feeling will get passed down," predicts Joan Hess.

Martin Ryan, the principal, explains how changes came about. "We went to parents in the Academic Boosters Club. We asked them what we could do to support their kids, and then we did it." Families said they didn't always feel comfortable in the schools, weren't happy with playgrounds, and didn't think of school as a "fun" place. Changes were made in playground equipment. Family recreational events were added. Kindergarten orientation events include storytelling in the library, athletic activities in the gym, and question-and-answer sessions with parents, teachers, and administrators.

Breaking the ice with families is vital. "I didn't volunteer in the classroom until after the first home visit," indicates Camille Butsic, a P.R.E.P.A.R.E. parent. "That made me more comfortable in getting to know the teacher and that she was human, not my boss or anybody to be afraid of. The next school year I started to volunteer right away. It

Home visits— with families of children ranging in age from birth through second grade—are a key component of many of our Initiatives to help families and schools prepare for each other.

Our Initiatives are learning to capitalize on each family's strengths rather than limit ourselves to overcoming barriers.

made me feel more comfortable, knowing what was going on and being part of everything, and feeling respected."

Families Rely on Support Networks

Nearly all families develop informal support networks, usually among neighbors, relatives, or friends. In today's mobile society, these networks—where childrearing concerns are resolved while sitting on the stoop or leaning over the fence—are more difficult to establish and maintain.

"Even stable, middle-class parents need to have their parenting skills validated," observes Sue Smith Aiken of Early Education Services. Parents As Teachers (PAT) is one of several strategies that enable families to share their ideas and become more confident about their parenting roles.

"What has made my experience with PAT so special has been the personal care shown towards me and my children," wrote one single parent. "I have no family.... Having the chance to speak with other parents...was very informative and comforting.... My little boy has made new friends and I have grown to feel more secure as a new mother."

Home Visits — A Personal Connection

Home visits, conducted by trained workers, reap many rewards for children, families, and teachers. Home visitors often serve as role models and links with the community.

New mothers often seek out the services of Project First Step. Its New Baby program relies on trained volunteers to visit new mothers in the hospital to provide information and answer questions. A mother who lived on a ranch 80 miles away from the hospital had her baby on the weekend, and was having problems with breastfeeding. "She was just desperate," recounts Jan McGinn. Reassuring advice enabled the mother to overcome her difficulties.

The PAT program through Early Education Services centers around home-based education services for parents of infants and preschoolers. This close contact enables home visitors to spot potential difficulties before they arise, and they help with everything from locating food to health care. "We're giving the moms a real sense of their abilities to teach their kids," says Carole Birch.

Families' experiences have often left them distrustful of school and human service officials. Home visitor Tammy Mallory, with Be-Four, finds that with patience and repeated home visits, she earns the parents' trust. Mallory remembers a family whose son was about to start kindergarten. The child, who had physical disabilities, needed transportation and special care during the school day. Mallory answered questions and addressed the family's concerns in detail. The mother visited her son's kindergarten class and talked with the other children to introduce her son and explain his medical condition.

"When you initiate those home visits, the benefits carry over into the class," finds Tom Brzezinski, a kindergarten teacher.

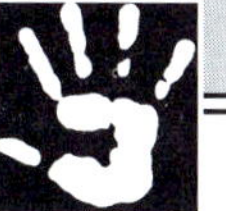

Assure Community Inclusiveness

Many families have no one to turn to. A Project First Step volunteer found a young mother in tears. “The family was packing to move, the baby was demanding to be fed every hour, and the young father was striding around impatiently slamming things in boxes,” recalls Marcia Simmons. “The volunteer asked to take the baby to her home. When she and the baby returned, the packing was done, mom and dad were once again calm and happy, and the baby had been fed every hour. The new parents were very grateful and insisted that Project First Step was wonderful and should be available everywhere.”

Several of our Initiatives help parents gain access to information and services. A computerized network makes it easier for PSCC families to sift through bureaucracy. Every elementary school in the city had expelled Raul. School officials insisted that his mother teach him at home. She needed to continue working to support her family. Counseling and tutoring staff coordinated efforts with the school district. Raul was helped to reach grade-level standards, made steady progress, and is doing well in sixth grade.

Families and teachers determine their own level of participation in P.R.E.P.A.R.E. “We try to make it as family-friendly as possible,” points out Mary Brien, superintendent of schools. “Family is really the focus: to make schools and parents partners.”

It takes an entire village
to raise a child.

–African proverb

Community inclusiveness—a commitment to young children that involves not only families and schools but business and civic life as well—is essential for children’s progress. “If you don’t have the community participation, your programs just won’t work,” states Lois Price of Success by Six.

Families Are Central to Communities

Families live, work, and play in communities. It only stands to reason, then, that communities that are truly committed to improving school preparation involve families. P.R.E.P.A.R.E.’s Mary Brien indicates, “We find that the real pressure for change comes…from the parents.”

How committed are families to changing the ways schools and children get ready for each other? P.R.E.P.A.R.E. parents who participate in a training program are given stipends to attend introductory

Assure Community Inclusiveness

- ***Families are central to communities.***
- ***Everyone creates the community’s vision.***
- ***Communities with vision support families.***

sessions with teachers. Many parents return the stipend. Their decision indicates the kind of high level of vision and commitment within communities that is typical when everyone supports children's success.

"We must re-create an attractive and caring attitude in our homes and in our worlds. If our children are to approve of themselves, they must see that we approve of ourselves." –Maya Angelou

Everyone Creates the Community's Vision

Each community, like every family, is unique. We urge you to take a good look at your community and school dynamics to spot challenges and opportunities. "You need to network for a long time before you set up [a program]. Get an idea of a community's strengths and weaknesses," advises Raquel Oliva of Avance. "This is not something you can force down into a community. It takes some time to get an idea of who a community's leaders are."

"In the first year we hired natural leaders who were respected within each community," explains Oliva. "The second year we filled vacancies with graduates of the Avance programs, which provided extensive job training and support. As a result, the program was never seen as an outsider."

"This isn't something you do *to* people. It's something you do *with* them," agrees Sue Smith Aiken of Early Education Services. Groundwork efforts include locating convenient meeting places, times, child care, and transportation. Ownership and involvement take shape when everyone works together to set, and find ways to achieve, the group's goals. The process requires a genuine commitment to community inclusiveness, not token gestures. In the long run, the rewards are worth the investment!

Communities that are truly committed to improving school preparation involve families in the process. Families and teachers focus on shared goals for children. We find that refreshments, transportation, convenient times and locations, and child care boost participation.

Community alienation with local education was tackled with a rousing start by the Pumsey Circuit Breaker, which "brought in a bluegrass band, invited neighborhood residents, parents, business people. The idea was for parents, grandparents, and area residents to have fun and see teachers more as human and approachable, and vice versa," relates Martin Ryan. "Parents and teachers got to see each other as neighbors and friends," he adds. "People need that sense of community. They need to feel they belong in that school."

Delta West uses a more traditional approach to community inclusiveness. A local advisory panel of residents and community leaders generates input into its efforts. The board, says Nancy Church, is extremely active and always full of ideas.

Sometimes a community knocks on the door. Thurston Woods Campus in Milwaukee is located in a refurbished church parish. By the time the school opened, former members of the parish were "dying to get a look at it," recalls Christine Burton-Maxwell. "The school had a big community lunch at the building, so everyone could come in and see it."

"We really tried to open doors to the community and, as a result, build on the strengths of the community," observes Dominic Gullo.

"Everyone wants to be involved. They just need a chance."

–Julia Krokstrom, parent, Iron Mountain, Michigan

Communities With Vision Support Families

What does it take to tap into a community's vision for success of children and schools? We find that it helps to be tenacious and to identify the right issues, approaches, and people.

Tammy Keiser is an enthusiastic parent whose second child is enrolled in KPEP. She is a literacy volunteer with parents and children. "The system keeps shoving these kids under the rug, because it doesn't have the time or the funds. It's pathetic, because you can see that these kids have bright minds," Keiser observes. "If we had more programs such as this, or Head Start…we wouldn't have a lot of the crime and problems later on."

Professional preparation enables teachers, home visitors, and other support staff to implement developmentally appropriate practices. "We provide ongoing inservice staff development as a major component. There is always something we need to know more about," acknowledges Martha Wheeler-Fair, principal at Frances Starms Early Childhood Center in Milwaukee.

Teachers with My Parent(s) and Me attended a National Black Child Development Institute conference.

They acquired information about learning styles of African American students, who make up more than 80 percent of the school's population, as well as other appropriate teaching techniques. "It was a wonderful experience for the staff, because they walked away saying things such as, 'Wow, that's why that kid does that!'" says Brendel Hatley, the school's principal.

Several of our schools open their doors to the community for special events and meals. Families and residents who feel they belong in the school are more likely to get involved in local education.

Professional preparation enables teachers, home visitors, and other support staff to implement developmentally appropriate practices. This student teacher is gaining hands-on classroom experience.

Business Involvement— One Way to Stretch Resources

Community commitment to families requires time, energy, and resources. Each business has its own needs and expectations. The direct sales approach seems to work best. "You really need to be able to…sell your concepts within about five minutes," according to P.R.E.P.A.R.E.'s Johanna Ostwald. "Get across how it's going to be mutually beneficial."

She notes that every business has a "budget that deals with community relations or public endeavors. We put together a very brief description—with graphics—of our goal. That is especially important when we are seeking a long-term commitment." Requests for specific items are made face to face. "They're parents, too, so you can really play on that," she says.

Pride and investment in the Initiative are promoted with "Family-Friendly Business Awards" given to businesses that offer resources. Certificates are signed by the school principal and parents. Donations include drinks and paper products for Pizza Night, lava rocks for night-sky bingo at the Family Night Under the Stars, and cash donations. The certificate is "a nice way to recognize their partnership," Ostwald comments.

One caution: Find out if there are any restrictions on donations. Three car dealers agreed to donate a minivan, but school officials could not accept it because "it didn't meet school bus safety standards," laments Sue Smith Aiken.

Ostwald points out that "The school neighborhood extends to the business community also. We live here, we work here, and business isn't a separate entity."

"You just go and ask," Aiken recommends. "Plead poverty, and talk about how your program will help children do better in school and help their parents complete school."

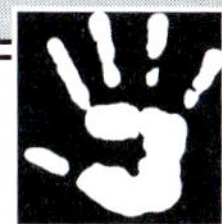

Promote Cultural Competence

Our Initiatives reach diverse populations in a variety of settings, yet without exception we are successfully preparing families and schools for each other. When our efforts are flexible, adaptable, and customized to families in our communities, we are far more likely to reach our goals. We find that what spurs one parent or community into action may threaten and alienate another. Some families and schools may be open to new ideas. Others are proud and are reluctant to accept "help," especially from outside agencies. "If a program's going to be successful, we have to mesh with the community's needs," observes Brendel Hatley, a principal in Battle Creek.

Know Your Community

To find out what kinds of approaches would fit your community, we recommend you become well versed about the area, its character, demographics, cultures, and history. Information about every community's characteristics is available through the Census Bureau, Head Start, and a variety of local agencies. Collect it. Analyze it. Decide what it means for your vision and efforts. Get to know the people, their needs and strengths. Then adapt accordingly.

Success By Six (SBS) serves three very different communities. Kashmere Gardens and Fifth Ward are primarily African American. About 95 percent of the mothers living there are single, and average an 11th-grade education. Denver Harbor is mostly Hispanic with 85 percent of its residents married. Many are immigrants from Mexico and South America with limited English-speaking abilities. The two areas also have many similarities: Both have high infant mortality rates, large numbers of low-birthweight babies, and many children who have difficulty in school.

> *"Once social change begins, it cannot be reversed. You cannot uneducate the person who has learned to read. You cannot humiliate the person who feels pride. You cannot oppress the people who are not afraid anymore."*
>
> –Cesar Chavez

How have our initiatives responded to community needs? Forms similar to Individualized Family Service Plans (IFSP) are used by Be-Four. Questions were changed several times at the request of families, and now the staff train others how to write IFSPs.

Recruiting reluctant families has been a challenge for many of us. Jan Fowler, director of Be-Four, offers these strategies to reduce barriers:

- Offer family-friendly, flexible arrangements. Make

Get to know the people in the community, their needs and strengths. Then adapt accordingly.

Program outreach services are far more effective when cultures in the community are treated with dignity and respect.

evening, late afternoon, early morning, or weekend appointments to accommodate work schedules. Meet somewhere other than the home if the family feels more comfortable.

- Ask an informal or formal support person to introduce you to the family. Familiar professionals such as teachers, public health nurses, and social service personnel can pave the way toward families they know. The initial visit could be in an agency office, for example.

She also offers evidence about the

Promote Cultural Competence

- ***Know your community.***
- ***Use culturally sensitive strategies and materials.***

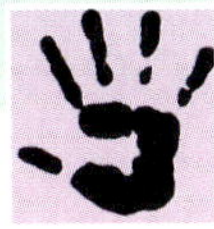

effectiveness of this approach. A family living far from the school was referred to Be-Four by an elementary principal. After initially agreeing to a home visit, the mother canceled at the last minute. The principal then made a personal introduction at a school event. This time, the family enrolled. Another family was referred by a kindergarten teacher. At the end of the third visit held at the school, the father felt comfortable enough to invite the home visitor to their home. A trusted social services agency staff member provided the link for another family, who stayed on for a second year with another child.

The Outdoor Learning Center at Post Elementary School attracts families with its array of hands-on activities for children and adults. In one instance, a mother and four children were confined to their home. The two oldest children had difficulty adjusting to kindergarten. During the year, the mother brought her younger children to the Outdoor Learning Center. These children had a much easier adjustment to kindergarten, and their mother became involved in PTA, school store, and classroom volunteering!

Sydney Martin, an Early Education Services Parent Educator, and a participating family celebrate Strawberry Thanksgiving by reading about it and enjoying fresh strawberries.

Use Culturally Sensitive Strategies and Materials

Community characteristics are addressed by successful school preparation programs in culturally-sensitive ways. It's really important to select staff who are part of the community and who speak the families' languages. Our printed materials reflect community characteristics, in words and pictures. Program outreach services are far more effective when cultures in the community are treated with dignity and respect.

Here's how SBS approached Kashmere Gardens, Fifth Ward, and Denver Harbor, according to Lois Price.

- A diverse group of employees and volunteers who share each community's cultural background was hired.
- With help from a professional and neighborhood marketing committee, Success by Six prepared a brochure published in both English and Spanish.

- In Kashmere Gardens, parent education classes are provided at a local school.
- Denver Harbor's program is offered at the Denver Harbor Community Center by the Avance-Houston program, which is familiar with the community. Through the parent education and home visiting programs, Avance provides a nurturing, culturally sensitive environment.
- Cultural holidays and customs are regularly incorporated into staff development and family activities.
- The Initiative is always looking for more information, improved ties to the community, and ways to adapt services.

Sensitivity to culture takes many forms. Strawberry Thanksgiving is celebrated in June by the Potawatomi and other Native American people in the Great Lakes area. It is a time to forgive, get in touch with one's feelings, and share time with family and friends. During a home visit with one Early Education Services family, a grandmother presented her granddaughter with a shawl she made for the child to dance in at her first official pow-wow.

Diversity and flexibility are cornerstones of success. Many of us began to offer child care and transportation for parenting classes. Others coordinate health care and housing assistance along with our preschool programs. As we learn more about the cultures in our community, we adjust our ideas accordingly.

Opening Doors—
In Housing Communities

Community acceptance and involvement in KPEP came slowly at first, recalls Mary Lindsey. "When we went door-to-door, we would hear music...but they still wouldn't open the door." To increase participation, parents who live in a Tampa housing community were enlisted to spread the word. A playground attracted children, who are only allowed to play there when accompanied by a parent.

"It's almost indescribable what's happening to the community," observes Lindsey. "Once they get into the program, really good things start to happen." Parents learn how to build on children's reading and learning skills as well as improve family relationships.

In addition, the Initiative worked with the Tampa Housing Authority to remodel its office and provide funding for residents to paint the housing development.

Establishing common ground with residents takes time. "It's not the sprint. It's the marathon. It's a matter of being there. We've come a long way in terms of trust," Lindsey realizes.

True preparation for life-long learning happens every day with families at home, in groups of young children,

and with the teachers and administrators in schools.

Engaging Your Community

"Demographics do not dictate destiny. Attitudes, leadership, and values do."

–Marian Wright Edelman

Families and communities go hand in hand when the goal is children's lifetime success. In this chapter, we share our recommendations for engaging the grassroots community in the quest for success.

Build on Community Assets

We know the value of customized services and integrated efforts into a broad spectrum of community—and in one initiative, entire state—resources and agencies. This comprehensive, long-term approach transforms mindsets. Many more people realize that true preparation for life-long learning happens every day with families at home, in groups of young children, and with the teachers and administrators in schools.

Our communities' greatest assets are people. Two things stretch as we build on what we have: Our vision of what it takes to achieve and maintain appropriate learning experiences and the human and financial resources to accomplish our vision.

"In the middle of every difficulty lies opportunity."

—Albert Einstein

Assess Your Community's Resources

What learning resources are available in your community or state? The search begins with a thorough look at every group or agency that touches the issues. Students of all ages, families, school personnel and resources, local officials, and human services usually head our lists. Sue Smith Aiken with Early Education Services recognizes that "one of the major functions our programs serve is to link families with community resources. Approximately 50 percent of staff time is spent on referrals. It is critical to collaborate with the wide variety of services for families."

Build on Community Assets

- ***Assess your community's resources.***
- ***Collaborate with local agencies and programs.***

Survey resources with an eye toward creating a network of people who can share ideas, support each other, and solve problems:

- local and state policymakers
- community and civic groups
- health care providers
- businesses
- colleges and universities
- Head Start, child care, family child care, and nursery schools
- national professional and service organizations
- state, county, and municipal agencies
- schools
- religious groups
- unions
- high school service learning programs

The possibilities are endless. Imagine how your initiative might extend, build upon, and perhaps even redirect each group's efforts.

What about fundraising to sustain your ideas? Bake sales can't generate the support needed to maintain a viable, comprehensive approach. Here's what some of us are doing.

Collaborate With Local Agencies and Programs

"We can get more bang for our buck if we collaborate and cooperate," contends Israel Tribble, Jr., President of the Florida Education Fund. "You're seeing more and more multiple-funded things that cross over and fertilize each other." He believes that "enlightened people in the public and private sectors must work together to mount a successful attack on the complex issues we face as a society."

Sharing resources, knowledge, and skills make it more likely that initiatives address both key issues:

- all the critical components that help children achieve their potential: health, nutrition, family and community stability, culture, self-esteem, and quality of early learning experiences
- all the areas in which schools can improve in their use of developmentally appropriate practices and curriculum content

Collaborations come in all shapes and sizes. They can be a tool to increase accessibility for families, to consolidate or upgrade services, or to arrange new services that would be impossible to provide otherwise.

- Success by Six helps families make connections with social service agencies, or arrange to have services offered at more convenient sites. "We collaborate, we coordinate, and we make the services accessible. If it's not accessible, the client won't participate," concludes Lois Price.
- "We don't have to reinvent the wheel. Use what others do. There's never enough money to replicate the infrastructure," advises Israel Tribble with KPEP. "The idea of building on a good base and taking it to the level you want to be at only makes good sense. Schools will never be able to provide all that needs to be supplied."
- Another approach for making the most of your community's assets is to restructure or build upon systems that affect schools and families. New programs are only one of the possibilities. In the Charlevoix-Emmet ISD,

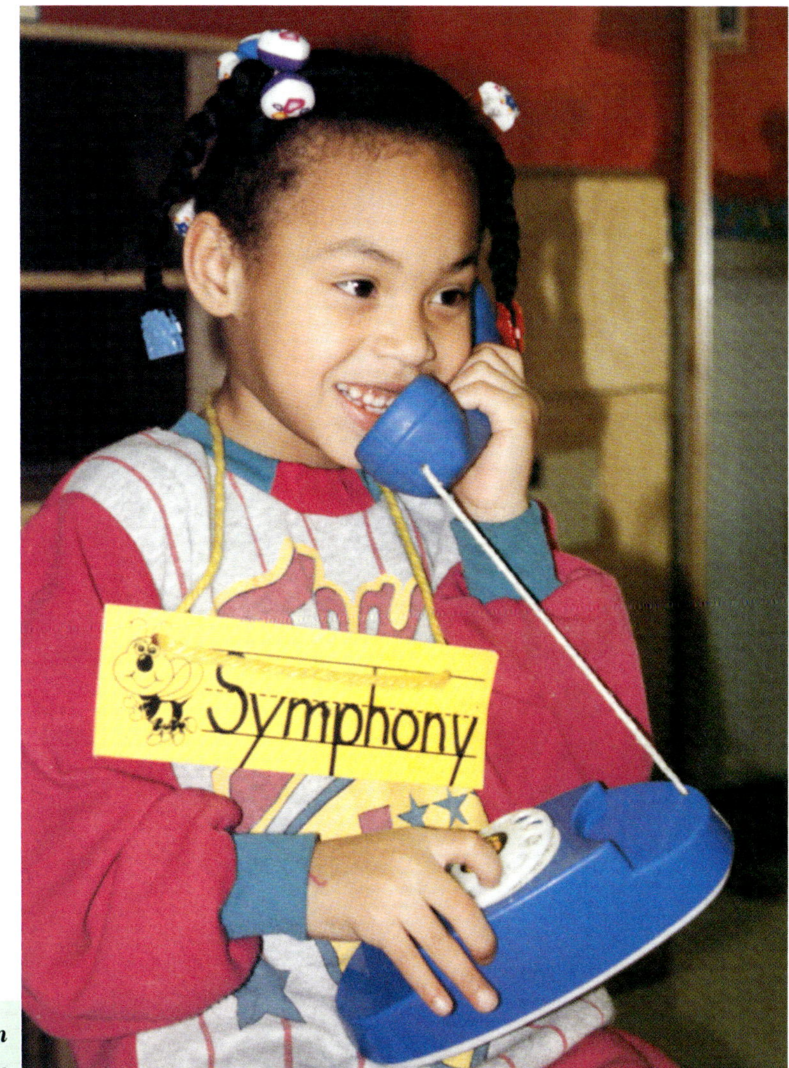

Success is within reach if you survey resources with an eye toward creating a network of people who can share ideas, support each other, and solve problems.

several small districts share teacher professional development opportunities—and everyone benefits.

- Several of us link with Head Start. Be-Four works with Head Start and other tuition-free preschools to jointly advertise services. "Collaborate! Collaborate!" encourages Jan Fowler. "Collaboration involves hard work and it takes time. A shared vision for the collaboration is a must."
- Avance brings information and connects services for participants by providing a community resource speaker during each class. Speakers are drawn from services such as the health department, nutrition education, family violence prevention, Planned Parenthood, public safety, and elected officials.
- Our most effective ideas are quickly incorporated into systems. P.R.E.P.A.R.E. is such a success that principal Scott McClure routinely quizzes job applicants about their willingness to make home visits and their ability to teach in developmentally appropriate ways.
- A communication network between Head Start and other early childhood programs, public service agencies, and private child care providers who serve low-income, working families was woven together by Early Education Services. A home visitor who spots an ear infection might refer the family to health care, to a specialist to treat a child's speech problem, or coordinate with the Department of Social Services to help stabilize the family.
- More formal collaboration, and an expanded age range for services, was achieved after a year of hard work by Early Education Services. The local Interagency Coordinating Council, required by the Individuals with Disabilities Act, dealt only with children from birth to age three. "We had to work with DSS, department heads, human service agencies. There are a lot of tough issues. You have to go the pace people are willing to change," indicates Sue Smith Aiken. After one year, the Interagency Coordinating Council expanded its focus to include services to all children in the preschool years, not just children birth to three with handicapping conditions. This expanded focus works better for all families.
- PSCC developed "one-stop shopping." Parents are interviewed by a counselor who feeds the information into the computer. Families learn immediately what social service programs, if any, they are eligible for, and the data is automatically processed on an application. This system reduces frustration by eliminating the social service maze. It puts families in touch with agencies that might be difficult to reach. As a result, more families in the school system receive services.

Paving the Way for Grassroots Collaboration

Most Kellogg Initiatives are local. The one exception is already making a difference locally. "We're trying to change the way state bureaucracy operates," says Linda McCart, program director at the National Governors' Association (NGA) Center for Policy Research. NGA's goal is to make it easier for grassroots people to be more creative in tackling school preparation issues.

The NGA is working with Colorado, Ohio, and South Carolina to find ways to streamline services and improve collaboration. Some tasks seem relatively simple. In one state, staff from the Departments of Social Services and Health were both routinely visiting new mothers in the hospital. Could the two departments coordinate their activities and arrange for only one visit?

The question raises a common hurdle to collaboration: turf battles. Consolidations might crimp staff levels and department budgets. "Whatever kind of collaboration or partnership you're trying to develop, it has to be a win-win situation for both parties," recognizes McCart.

She is optimistic that the goal is worth the effort. Ohio is fundamentally reforming the way children's services are governed, delivered, and financed through the Family and Children First Initiative. Only 9 counties of the 88 in the state could be funded, but 45 others are moving ahead on their own. The first step is to identify state and federal barriers to comprehensive services. Some counties are working on structural reorganization. Others pool funding in order to serve children who do not meet federal eligibility requirements. Still others improved access to services. Ohio "had a lot of health care services, but no one was using them because they were hard to get to. So they moved a clinic into a church basement, and it's open at night, and the clients love it." In order for the clinic to meet regulations from various agencies and departments, state officials collaborated. Another county moved the child welfare agency into school administrative offices. Successes in Ohio demonstrate that state and local reform efforts can be accomplished when partners collaborate.

McCart's philosophy is this: "Instead of duplicating services, think: restructure. Think: instead of, not: in addition to. My other advice is: Don't take 'No' for an answer when a state says something can't be done."

Elizabeth Stief, a policy analyst at the NGA Center for Policy Research, agrees. "A lot of the barriers that people think exist, really don't."

Collaborations can be a tool to increase accessibility for families, to consolidate or upgrade services, or to arrange new services that would be impossible to provide otherwise.

Work for Results

"I long to accomplish a great and noble task, but it is my chief duty to accomplish small tasks as if they were great and noble."

–Helen Keller

What could be more abstract—and broader in scope—than the concept of preparing schools and children for each other? We learned that in order to successfully tackle an abstract idea, we need concrete goals and indicators of progress.

Know What You Want to Achieve

Before your community chooses your goals, review the critical contributors to children's success, and keep in mind that families and schools are partners. Make sure, too, to set realistic, achievable goals.

Integrate systems, and build on what's already in place. Sustain your gains. Aim higher next year!

What can you do in your community to be sure that schools and families are prepared for, and continue to support, each other? You might ask questions such as these:

- *How well does the primary curriculum reflect current research about developmentally appropriate practice?*
- *What information do parents of newborns seek?*
- *Are kindergarten entry requirements fair and appropriate?*
- *Can all young children receive their immunizations?*
- *How could neighborhood stability be increased?*
- *What instills a love of reading in young children?*
- *How could community awareness about the importance of children's early experiences be raised?*

Work for Results

- ***Know what you want to achieve.***
- ***Specify indicators of success.***
- ***Focus on your goals.***

Specify Indicators of Success

How do we know when we're making progress and have achieved our goals? We set both short-term and long-range goals. Exactly how we measure success influences our structure and approach, so we are selective.

We look for both subjective and objective ways to measure the effects of our efforts. You can, too. For instance, if you're planning to increase immunization levels of preschoolers, your rate of success will depend on current immunization levels. If 50 percent of preschoolers are immunized now, you might aim for 75 percent the first year, and 90 percent the next—remember, new babies are always being born.

How to track progress and results? Document which groups collaborate to recruit families and provide services. Log how many doses of each vaccine are given. Along with medical records, collect comments from parents, child care providers, and teachers about the peace of mind gained by knowing children are protected.

Some results can be measured or recorded on paper; others are less tangible. We use questionnaires, interviews, photographs, attendance records, evaluations, and other methods to collect information that matches our goals.

Listen for heartfelt testimonials. "I want to be a good teacher," reflects Merry Hall. "If you want to be good you have to take some risks. I did not have parents in my room, not that they weren't welcome, but opening that door was a hard step. I feel that I'm a better teacher because they're involved."

Keep in mind that families and schools are partners. Make sure, too, to set realistic, achievable goals. Integrate systems, and build on what's already in place.

that door was a hard step. I feel that I'm a better teacher because they're involved."

Document progress regularly, rather than waiting for the end of the project to do an evaluation. "There's a lot that we're learning" about the most effective strategies for each community, acknowledges Raquel Oliva, of Avance. Many adjustments are made as programs evolve, to respond to circumstances before it's too late.

Some indicators of success are evident primarily with children. In Broken Bow, Nebraska, home visits began for a mother and her infant who was failing to thrive. Project First Step could soon measure the results—the baby started gaining weight at the rate of two pounds a week!

Avance measures success with questionnaires and interviews. The 1994 evaluation documents contained these remarkable outcomes for the program in the Rio Grande Valley:

- Parents increased their knowledge of child development and parenting skills.
- Parents reported more nurturing attitudes toward their children.
- Parents had a greater appreciation of their role as teachers of their children.
- Parents reported less severe attitudes regarding punishment.
- 100% of the mothers contacted were interested in continuing in the family literacy program.

At Milwaukee's Frances Starms Early Childhood Center, an integrated, developmentally appropriate curriculum is offered. New assessment procedures necessitated a redesign of the progress reporting system. Teachers, specialists, and parents observe each child, record behaviors, and describe the child's developmental and academic status.

"Child Development Day" is held at Thurston Woods Campus, also part of the Milwaukee Initiative. Parents bring their children, ages birth to five, for comprehensive screening. A play-based assessment follows parent interviews. Each family completes a survey to determine if it would benefit from community services. Representatives are on hand to answer questions.

Increased educational involvement by families is another indicator of effectiveness. Martin Ryan, principal at J.W. Mauck, home of the Pumsey Circuit Breaker, tells this story. Two years ago, one couple was "leery of the school, viewed the PTO with suspicion, and was adamantly opposed to a PTO fundraiser. They were invited to attend PTO meetings and family-oriented events." The father now spearheads PTO fruit basket sales, and in a recent radio interview, proudly stated, "At Mauck, we're always looking for ways to make it a place for the family, not just the students."

The critical value of sustaining children's

At Frances Starms Early Childhood Center, teachers, specialists, and parents observe each child, record behaviors, and describe the child's developmental and academic status.

where youth from ages 10 to 14 come to see themselves as achievers. Donnell, a 12-year-old, was reading on a first-grade level and printed and wrote in cursive with difficulty. Through arts and crafts experiences to develop his fine motor skills, his writing and drawing abilities greatly improved. Donnell writes,

> *In the past, I was a mischievous child. I use[d] to get into fights…I disobeyed rules…I just didn't care.*
>
> *Just recently I realized I had potential and talent and decided I had to get my act together. I want to show myself I can do almost anything if I put my mind to it to achieve my goals. With my knowledge I can also show others you can do good if you put your heart and mind to it. From my troubled times,*

Many adjustments are made as programs evolve, to respond to circumstances before it's too late.

I progressed fast. I am a Boy Scout leader. I take part in…Staying Ahead Leadership. We get to meet different people from all walks of life such as political leaders and doctors. We do go places I've never dreamed of. I can show others there is more to life than just fun and games."

Youth Workers at Staying Ahead consistently instill the message that "Your educational destiny is not left up to chance, but rather it is a matter of choice."

Focus on Goals

Flexibility is essential to stay focused on our goals. No matter how well planned our efforts, there are always details to work out, new information to absorb, and changes to incorporate.

The National Governors' Association is helping one state change policies for its Family Resource Center program. At first, the state didn't want to dictate an excessive number of policies and procedures. Officials soon learned that not enough direction was being

Success—Many Facets

Cindy was a 23-year-old mother with a first-grader, Sonny, and 10-month-old Susie. She had no phone or car, survived on Aid to Families with Dependent Children (AFDC), and had one friend in the trailer park in rural Michigan. Cindy knew about Parents As Teachers (PAT), offered through Early Education Services, but was afraid of what would be said about Susie, who had just learned to roll over, but did not sit up or crawl. She had no verbalization and her eyes were crossed.

Cindy first met a PAT parent educator at her friend's home. PAT linked Susie with health care professionals for her eyes, low weight, and anemic condition. Eventually, Susie was diagnosed as a Fetal Alcohol Syndrome baby. Sonny, considered the "man of the house" because his mom had just kicked out another abusive boyfriend, suffered from headaches, and was not doing well in school. PAT arranged for a social work intern to talk with him, and Sonny loved his new friend; they met once a week during the school year.

Cindy moved out of the school district three times, but reconnected with PAT each time she moved back. Jessie was born when Susie was 2 1/2 years old. Cindy had moved in with another abuser, but expressed a heartfelt desire to break this pattern of domestic assault. PAT linked her with a women's center and Cindy was on the road to making positive changes in her life.

At age 3, Susie entered a group program. She blossomed in her peer interactions and her language growth. A special education home visitor brought activities and information on parenting for Cindy. Of the weekly home visits, Cindy commented, "They are the best quality time I spend with my kids. We all look forward to them so much. I think my kids will be ready for school—they just learn so many things."

Cindy has now found a job, a reliable child care provider, and housing. She hopes to go to college and become a social worker. Looking back, Cindy asks, "What would I have done if the parent educator hadn't come into our lives? I wouldn't have known all the problems Susie had. She needed all that special help. PAT was the best thing that ever happened to us!"

At the age of 7, Cindy's oldest child, Sonny, is thriving in his role as big brother to Jessie.

Flexibility is essential to stay focused on our goals. No matter how well planned our efforts, there are always details to work out, new information to absorb, and changes to incorporate.

provided for the initiatives to succeed, explains Linda McCart. "Now we're trying to help them fix that and make mid-course corrections," she indicates.

Battle Creek schools continue to adjust to changing conditions. A key organizer took another position, and three of the four schools hired new principals. The neighborhoods include many rental properties and families relocate often, so principals expect to periodically redo the family survey to stay in tune with populations.

By keeping in touch with exactly what is happening within our Initiatives, we celebrate our progress and adjust components accordingly.

Preparation of Adults— Working Toward Collaboration

Parents and educators alike are being reached through the Milwaukee Early Schooling Initiative at Frances Starms Early Childhood Center and Thurston Woods Campus, both new public schools.

Family Centers are now integral to both programs, and a place to "consider yourself at home." At Frances Starms, parents browse through materials, ask the parent coordinator questions, and talk with other families. Family members are encouraged to visit their children's classrooms and to borrow materials from the lending library. Workshops and "make-it-and-take-it" activities are offered on topics such as child development, parenting, curriculum, and community issues. Parent-infant-toddler groups are forming. A grandparent support group was formed for older family members who provide extensive child care.

In addition to these hubs of activities, families are an integral part of implementing Frances Starms' new developmentally appropriate assessment process. "The key to all of this is recognizing we all have to work together, and to give up the notion that schools or families can educate children on their own," states Dominic Gullo, professor at the University of Wisconsin-Milwaukee.

Professional Development Centers are another component. Teachers, administrators, community agency personnel, and families were asked what they needed to know about young children. Now they're learning about what they asked for, under the tutelage of public school teachers, university professors, and community agencies. "We're finding teachers who are incredibly innovative and more than willing to wipe the slate clean," observes Christine Burton-Maxwell, another UMW faculty member. Frances Starms and Thurston Woods staff also meet with each other and teachers at three other elementary schools to assure continuity with children's earlier experiences through a regular exchange of information and ideas.

Student teachers are increasing their professional preparation in a similar program. "Student [teachers] who go there are getting some really great training," indicates Gullo.

Find Partners

- ***Consider all possibilities.***
- ***Seek human and financial resources.***

Think how much more we can accomplish if we view parents, residents, businesses, and others as valuable partners!

Find Partners

We know that it pays to work together. We are pooling financial and human resources to more effectively serve our communities. We've found that we can count not only on the usual supports, but that many untapped resources can be instrumental.

Partnerships take time. Jan Fowler with Be-Four reveals that their referral system took three years to develop. Health care providers, schools, social services, religious organizations, and the local media are all instrumental in reaching out to the community.

Early Education Services markets its accomplishments with the goal of developing constant funding streams. Respite care was piloted. A contract was reached with the Department of Social Services to provide parent education. College students are involved in rural health fairs and regularly work with staff and families.

> *"Perseverance is not a long race; it is many short races one after another."*
>
> –Walter Elliott

Consider All Possibilities

Regular standbys are excellent sources of support for new ventures. Think how much more we can accomplish if we view parents, residents, businesses, and others as valuable partners! Kindergarten teacher Merry Hall is enthusiastic. "Getting parents involved is one of the best things we can do because it makes the school more of a family unit, more a community. Wouldn't it be great if this became nationwide? And it doesn't cost any money!"

Resources in our own backyards make it possible to direct limited funds to the most effective use. Avance relies on community resources to increase its services. Program sites are provided by the Boys and Girls Club in McAllen; a grassroots organization, Unidos Podemos, provides the facility in Linda Vista; and Starr County provides the facility in La Casita. A van was donated by a local grocery store chain.

Seek Human and Financial Resources

Much more than money is involved in contributing to success with school readiness. Tracy Nofs, principal of Coburn School which has a Student Readiness Program, learned, "I can't always look at resources as money. When we can see parents and community residents as resources, we're going to go a lot further."

Initially, Project First Step relied on volunteers. Project Coordinator Marcia Simmons provided information to new mothers in the hospital. Interested mothers were assigned to a compatible volunteer for continuing contact. Simmons cautions, however, that "volunteers quickly burn out, and too much staff time and expense is required for retraining." Hiring and training paraprofessionals is recommended.

Mary Lindsey with KPEP agrees, and suggests hiring people who at least "have a high school diploma or equivalent, some evidence of volunteer work, and some knowledge of the population."

You, too, can spot the opportunities in your community. Dovetail with each other to grow. Use your imagination. Instead of reinventing the wheel, give an old idea a new twist and take it further.

Unexpected New Partners—Project Educational Impact (PEI)

Roger Witherbee thought he received a chilly reception when he talked to local business people about school preparation. Imagine how pleased he was when the group helped generate $27,000 in donations!

Witherbee began looking for PEI supporters in his rural area, which has high unemployment rates. His search for collaborators led him to the Community Foundation for Northeast Michigan, whose focus was "Making It Happen in the Community."

Witherbee went to a breakfast meeting of business people "and gave an overview of our PEI program and…maybe spent 10 minutes answering some questions. They didn't seem too interested," he says. "But after the meeting I talked to a couple of the people and they were fired up."

Witherbee was asked to give a presentation to the Community Foundation's board of directors, and felt better about the results of this meeting. "What happened is these guys went out and started beating the bushes (for donations)." Altogether, about $27,000 poured in from a local church foundation, individuals, businesses, and the foundation.

Another collaborative effort involves the public agency that operates Head Start in nine northern Michigan counties. The agency now serves as fiscal agent for PEI, who is looking to expand into another school and to build even more partnerships. "We want every child [who can benefit from PEI's services] to be identified at day one, with follow-up for 5 years," he stresses. "We can't begin to meet all the needs. But there is a real exciting willingness to work collaboratively."

Tell Everybody

"A mind stretched by new ideas never returns to its original dimensions."

–Oliver Wendell Holmes

We're spreading the word about preparing families and schools for each other! Networking with the "choir" of those who understand the concept and reaching out to the community are both essential. Keep communication channels open and be alert to new possibilities. As each of us devised a communication plan, we took a close look at the dynamics of our areas. We figured out how to make communication work for us. Now we collect newsletters, brochures, clippings, and pass on the information.

Network With Supporters

Child care providers, Head Start, school personnel, and related professionals are keenly interested in children's futures. Delta West requires staff to spend half of their time in the community with physicians, principals, school nurses, pharmacists, and other professionals, notes Nancy Church. "We think it's real important that you make contacts before problems happen," she notes. Many of us now extend such contacts to state and national levels.

Linda McCart, with Creating Collaborative Frameworks, urges that project leaders, "Have a cup of coffee with your peer at the Department of Education. You can get more done over a cup of coffee than if you launch a major initiative and go to the legislature for funding." Networking within the profession spirals the effects of our work, and "it's just a matter of being creative and reaching out."

Tell Everybody

- ***Network with supporters.***
- ***Generate publicity.***

We heartily recommend extending an arm to policymakers—school boards, legislatures, municipal governments—to increase the likelihood for sustainability and expansion.

We heartily recommend extending an arm to policymakers—school boards, legislatures, municipal governments—to increase the likelihood for sustainability and expansion. "Big shots" such as school board presidents, state legislators, county commissioners, and the head of the Department of Social Services in Allegan County, Michigan, went on home visits during Legislators Day for the Month of the Young Child to get a close-up view.

"We're on the cutting edge of doing things differently, and happy to be a part of it" indicates Joyce Taylor, principal of Thurston Woods Campus. "Parents are enthusiastic. They tell other parents about the excitement and energy."

Generate Publicity

People can be ardent supporters—but they need to know about us! Continuous publicity, highlighting local success, is a sure winner. Direct mail and cable television are preferred by the Pumsey Circuit Breaker. "We need to make sure this isn't kept under a basket," says Martin Ryan. Community television stations are eager to run short videos about local events. Joann Hess recommends learning how to shoot the most effective material.

Be-Four uses flyers, news releases, and a brochure to advertise. Jan Fowler presents sessions at professional conferences such as the Michigan Association for the Education of Young Children, the National Rural Education Association, and the Michigan Department of Education. Be-Four received national attention when it was highlighted in "Transitions to School" published by the National Governors' Association in 1994.

Nebraska's governor honored Project First Step by designating it as a Good Beginnings program to encourage communities to educate and support families. First Lady Diane Nelson presented a plaque to First Step in August 1994. "Project First Step—Good Beginnings Week" was celebrated with cookies and conversation.

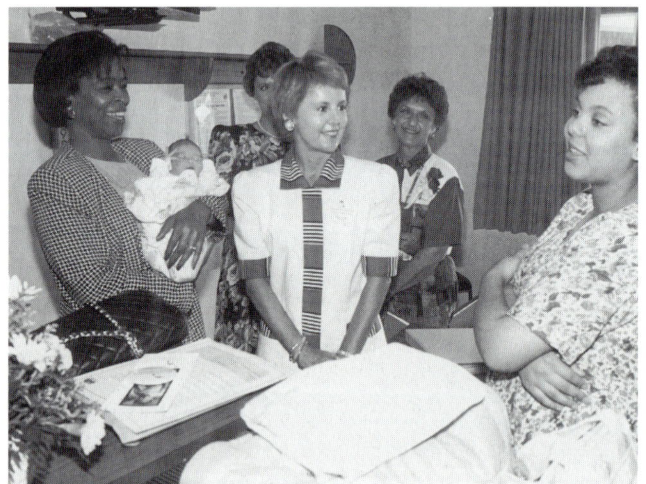

Project First Step was honored by the governor of Nebraska as a Good Beginnings program. Mary Dean Harvey, Director of the state's Department of Social Services, holds new baby Taylor Blanchard. First Lady Diane Nelson, visits with new mother Naomi Blanchard. Project First Step staff observe.

Create a Bigger Dream

"The future belongs to those who believe in the beauty of their dreams."

–Eleanor Roosevelt

Our goal is to assist children, families, and schools to prepare for each other. As you decide how to tackle the challenge, remember that well-informed families and professionals are our strongest advocates. When you nurture local leadership skills, you are one step closer to promoting children's success.

Develop Advocates for Families and Schools

Parents are the child's best advocate," notes one participant. Families who understand the issues are in a better position to make decisions about parenting and their children's education.

- *Tammy Keiser, a participant in KPEP, is a regular school volunteer. "Education is the most important thing we could give our children," she says. "I want to help them avoid what their moms went through.... I want to see these kids go to college."*
- *Gloria Rodriguez, of Avance sees the value of preparing parents "to be leaders and hold officials accountable. That has helped mobilize county government to act. [Parents] go from having no knowledge or support, and some despair, to going beyond their role as parents and teaching kids to help themselves." Raquel Oliva adds that "people have great aspirations for their children. They come to our program because they want their children to succeed."*
- *"Parents become volunteers in the classrooms and, after class, they start giving me opinions and offering ideas," indicates teacher Tom Brzezinski. "I have more outspoken parents now, not in an aggressive way, but in an assertive way. It's wonderful."*

Dream

- ***Develop advocates who lead families and schools to be prepared for each other.***

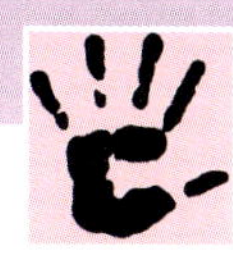

Advocacy is common among families who are empowered to speak up on behalf of their children. Four parents—a father, two teen mothers, and another

A Free-Standing Public Relations Tool in Battle Creek

Children, families, and community residents are flocking to the grounds of Post Elementary School in Battle Creek. What's the attraction?

An Outdoor Learning Center, complete with a track for children's riding vehicles, was built adjacent to the kindergarten classroom at part of its School Readiness Initiative. One portion of the area is covered for year-round play. Families and children stop by regularly to play, garden, or attend classes together. Activities range from outdoor safety to making bird feeders. A police officer demonstrated how traffic lights work.

"It just puts a little green spot in the school scene," says Suzanne Cumings, the teacher, about what she calls a free-standing public relations tool. "It helps kids get used to the school building. Also, the parents get to know us and feel comfortable with us before the first day."

mother—proudly testified about the value of Early Education Services' efforts in state hearings.

Educators are also learning and applying more about what it takes to prepare themselves to nurture success. The Milwaukee Early Schooling Initiative exemplifies a comprehensive approach. "We believe that a 'bottom-up' process builds upon existing strengths," explains Christine Burton-Maxwell. "We have to be responsive to families in a different way than we have been," she urges, "and to somehow think beyond academic achievement to include other aspects of children's lives. That's necessary if we are going to have children who can achieve long-term success."

"It's fun to work here!" exclaims Martha Wheeler-Fair, principal at Frances Starms Early Childhood Center. The program creates "a more productive environment for us, so children benefit from that. Parents are elated. They have grown to understand what our program has done with children." What is her vision? "We all want it to exist for children beyond this building, for kindergarten through grade 12."

"Kids are growing by leaps and bounds because of the continuity between families, child care providers, and our school."

–Martha Wheeler-Fair, principal, Frances Starms Early Childhood Center, Milwaukee, Wisconsin

Our Kellogg Foundation Initiatives—individuals and organizations—are forging new leadership tools to assure that schools and families are prepared for each other. We are investing in each child's future. How will you join us with your own grassroots success?

Which School? — Helping Milwaukee Families Decide

Knowledge is vital in Milwaukee, where the school district allows families to choose their children's schools. Each building has a different approach, so it's important for families to make an informed judgment about which is most appropriate for their child.

The Milwaukee Early Schooling Initiative based at Frances Starms Early Childhood Center offers programs for children from ages 3 through 6. Information about the various school curriculums is collected and shared with families. Parents are helped to understand their own child's development. When faced with a decision about enrollment in an elementary school, families are better prepared to make the choice.

The project also includes a "feeder" school network. The early childhood center works with staff at four other elementary schools to assure continuity with children's earlier experiences. Although parents are not required to send their children to these schools, the consistent curriculum is quite appealing. Staff from the programs engage in professional development activities together and regularly exchange information and ideas.

Schools and Families – Preparing Together

The W.K. Kellogg Foundation School Readiness Initiatives

Infants and toddlers. Rural, suburban, urban. Preschoolers and school-agers. Families. Teachers and principals. Community volunteers. Agencies and businesses. Colleges.

Our Kellogg Foundation Initiatives touch a wide variety of settings and populations. We're tackling the challenge of preparing schools and families for each other in a diversity of ways. These vivid sketches capture the flavor of what we are accomplishing. Initiatives are presented in alphabetical order by our names. Five elementary schools in Battle Creek, Michigan, are included, all of which are part of the district's broad efforts. Six Initiatives were funded through the National Association for the Education of Young Children, each of which is indicated separately as well.

As you read about us, we encourage you to look for similarities to your community's goals, strengths, and challenges. We're making a difference, and you can, too. Still have questions? We're always delighted to share our enthusiasm about what we're learning. Just call us!

Avance-Rio Grande Valley
National Association for the Education of Young Children / Goal One Project

Agency
Avance, Inc.

Contacts
Gloria Rodriguez
President/CEO, Avance, Inc.
301 S. Frio Suite 310
San Antonio, TX 78207
210-270-4630 / Fax 210-270-4612
Raquel Oliva
Executive Director, Avance-Rio Grande Valley
808 S. Main
McAllen, TX 78501
210-618-1642 / Fax 210-618-1698

Population
Low-income Hispanic families living in the Rio Grande Valley in three distinct communities: McAllen–a small city; Linda Vista–a colonia or rural subdivision lacking basic services; La Casita–an older rural farming community. Many participants are immigrants–67% were born in Mexico but have lived in the U.S. an average of 10 years. Average formal education is less than 7 years; 33% have a high school diploma or equivalent. Families have low incomes–57% have annual incomes of less than $6,000. Unemployment is high–41% have no employed parent at time of enrollment. Most–70%– are married. Most households–65%– speak only Spanish.

Initiatives
Strengthen families through community-based comprehensive services designed to prevent educational problems and child abuse and neglect; help families stabilize their economic situation; and encourage children and parents to reach their full potential.

Parents and children's programs offered in English and Spanish meet once a week for 3 hours for 9 months. Topics in the parenting program include child growth and development, nutrition, health, discipline, language, and the basic needs of children. Parents make educational toys for use as home teaching tools. While parents attend classes, birth to 4-year-old children take part in an early childhood education program designed to stimulate learning and language development and help ease the children's transition into school. Transportation is available for families to attend the program as well field trips to the library, zoo, and community events.

Home visits are video taped for self-observation and are designed to encourage parent-child interaction using educational toys made by the parent. A family literacy program is offered to graduates of the program.

Successes
Parents demonstrate an increased knowledge in parenting skills and are more likely to see themselves as teachers of their children. At the end of the program year, 100% of the participants expressed satisfaction with their experiences at Avance. Noelia Lopez indicates, "I am a different person. Now I am studying and working as a teacher aide. I am attending GED classes and have taken the GED tests. I never planned to study or work before Avance."

Mothers in the program indicated increased feelings of nurturance toward their children and were less likely to express strict attitudes about discipline and severe punishment. One mother explains that she spanked her older children, but now realizes "that praising children gives me better results than getting after them."

Be-Four School Project

Agency
Charlevoix-Emmet Intermediate School District
P.O. Box 318
Mercer Boulevard
Charlevoix, MI 49720
616-547-9947 / Fax 616-547-5621

Contacts
Jan Fowler, Director, Early Education Consortium
Tammy Mallory, Home Visitor, Be-Four School Project

Population
Eleven school districts that serve 10,460 students across 1,105 square miles in rural northern Michigan, including an island 32 miles offshore in Lake Michigan. Serves between 75 and 100 families with children ages 3 and 4 each year. Most of the families are white, and about 80% have low incomes. Risk factors include unemployment, low education, high family density, substance abuse, and single parenthood.

Initiatives
Develop a comprehensive method to smooth transition from preschool into kindergarten. Throughout year, home visitors provide developmentally appropriate activities for children, and increase parent knowledge and skill in nurturing the growth and development of their child. As school entry nears, families and their home visitors plan visits to the classroom, discussion of school expectations, preparation for changes in routines, a meeting with other Be-Four families and the elementary principal, and a home visit from the kindergarten teacher.

Families and home visitors prepare a document similar to the Individual Family Service Plan. The form has been revised several times to be more user-friendly in assisting the home visitor and family to identify needs, implement actions, and evaluate progress towards individual goals.

Collaborative recruitment with Head Start and other tuition-free preschool programs. All parties agreed to the goals and process for arrangement. Staff place as many eligible children as possible in each program. Agencies continue to work together throughout the year.

Expand services to include families with 3-year-old children and center-based programs housed in elementary school buildings. Participating school districts have increased from 3 to 10. Five new center programs for 4-year-olds opened in fall 1994.

Successes
Tailor individual goals to family needs and wishes. One family was concerned about their son's speech. When testing showed that his speech was appropriate for his age, the "stress level about their child was greatly reduced and they were able to spend more time working with him on different areas."

Connect families to formal and informal support. A formerly isolated parent notes that she is "dieting, looking into area churches, meeting with friends a little more often, and making lots of plans."

Increase children's capacity to benefit from kindergarten. One home visitor indicates that "Barbie began the Be-Four program with a short attention span, few limits on her behavior, and limited socialization experiences. She has been exposed to a variety of experiences that have made her potential shine this year. She enjoyed interacting with other adults and children at groups and is comfortable separating from mom. Barbie received the dental assistance that she needed."

Expand parent knowledge and skill in nurturing their children's growth. One mother has more appropriate expectations and asks more open-ended questions, observes a home visitor.

Strengthen parent-child interaction. One father indicated, "I've been trying to stick to it with my son on steady discipline and trying to spend more quality time with him. Also trying to be more considerate to my wife."

Facilitate service integration and communication among agencies. Irregular work hours for one mother created difficulty in establishing a consistent routine for her son. The Be-Four team asked her employer to give her reduced and regular hours. "The restaurant manager willingly provided" a better schedule. Be-Four purchases counseling services, physicals, dental appointments, eye exams, and respite care for families who have nowhere else to turn.

Promote positive parent-school relationships. A mother was very negative about school with an older child. After a year of experience working with school personnel, she began the next year on a more positive note.

Creating Collaborative Frameworks for "School Readiness"

Agency
National Governor's Association
Children and Social Services Program
444 N. Capitol Street, N.W., Suite 267
Washington, DC 20001-1572
202-624-5300 / Fax 202-624-5313

Contacts
Linda McCart, Program Director
Elizabeth Stief, Policy Analyst

Population
Young children in the states of Colorado, Ohio, and South Carolina.

Initiatives
Seeks to build the capacity for systemic change in social services, health, education, mental health, and early childhood development programs. Strategies include:

- analyze each state's services for young children and provide extensive on-site technical assistance
- create a network of state and local policymakers to facilitate problem solving, to provide peer support, and to share lessons learned
- identify specific federal and state barriers to integrated, comprehensive services for young children
- develop strategies and specific action plans to eliminate and/or reduce the identified barriers
- create state policy, regulatory, financial, and accountability frameworks to allow local communities to establish integrated, comprehensive service systems for young children and their families

Successes
States developing strategies to overcome challenges identified through site visits and analyses of services.

Significant progress in creating policy frameworks for preparing schools and families for each other. States explore strategies for new financial systems for integrated services. Agency directors meet regularly to coordinate efforts and discuss various issues and potential solutions. Teams of mid-level agency managers help implement systemic reform, identify problems, craft workable solutions, and improve relationships with counties and communities.

States working to reform at least one federal program for children in order to deliver services more effectively and to be more responsive to children and families.

Communities in each state included in implementation of comprehensive services for young children.

Delta West Community-Based Project
National Association for the Education of Young Children / Goal One Project

Agency
Children's Medical Services
P.O. Box 11427, Slot 526
Little Rock, AR 72203
501-682-8224, 1001 / Fax 501-682-8247

Contacts
Nancy Church, R.N., Administrator

Population
Four counties in the Arkansas Delta. Target is children with special needs; about two-thirds of the children are African American, most of the others are white.

Initiatives
Make home visits to increase families' access to agencies and parenting skills, and encourage job training and education for parents.

Coordinate with Kids First health services, special health care, and developmentally appropriate education for children up to age 3. Families receive parenting education and transportation.

Successes
More than twice as many children with special health care needs are being served since the initiative started; two more offices are opening.

Transportation is provided to medical clinics and parent support group meetings.

A representative is an active member of the Children's Medical Service Parent Advisory Council.

Social worker is involved with parent education and preparing Individual Family Service Plans and Individual Education Plans for children and families.

Early Education Services for Parents, Infants, and Preschoolers

Agency
Allegan County Intermediate School District
Early Education Services
310 Thomas Street
Allegan, MI 49010
616-673-2161
or
Plainwell Community Schools
600 School Drive
Plainwell, MI 49080
616-685-2094 / Fax 616-685-1108

Contact
Sue Smith Aiken, Early Education Services Director
Carole Birch, Parent Educator

Population
Seven school districts covering 850 square miles in rural southwest Michigan. Population is 90,500 with 3% Hispanic, 1% African American, less than 1% Native American. Approximately 50% of families are considered to be at high risk: 19% poverty, 27% illiteracy rate, high rate of child abuse and neglect. No public transportation. In 1993-94, 280 children received early education services.

Initiatives
Parents As Teachers (PAT) home-based education for parents, infants, and preschoolers. Emphasizes family goals and strengths.

Early childhood education information and referrals to school and community resources. Preschools for 4-year-olds at risk.

Play groups for parents and preschoolers each month in each school district. Offer

activities including family literacy, health, and fun.

Parent support/education groups offered at least twice a year in each district. Classes on child discipline run from 6 to 8 weeks. Seminars offered regularly on high interest topics such as children of divorce or Attention Deficit Disorder.

Even Start for high school dropout parents and their young children in Plainwell School District. Activities include breakfast, lunch, child care, time to play together, cooking, field trips, swimming, music, library visits, crafts. Parents complete high school while 3- and 4-year olds are in preschool.

Successes

Hired Parent Educators who are Native American and bilingual to offer special programming to diverse families. Retention rate in PAT is 90%. PAT is certified by the National Diffusion Network as being valid and replicable.

Grant to implement Healthy Families America to serve families at severe risk of child abuse, and a Respite Care contract with the Department of Social Services.

Provide home-based, school-linked services for children with developmental delays or disabilities. Implemented inclusion classroom for pre-primary children with impairments and educationally at-risk four-year-olds.

Engage in joint recruiting with Head Start.

Link families with community resources. Expanded the Part H Interagency Coordinating Council to coordinate all preschool activities in the county. Involves more than 20 agencies in a seamless continuum of services.

Effective Parent Training and Education Program

National Association for the Education of Young Children / Goal One Project

Agency

Southwest Communication Resources, Inc.
P.O. Box 788
Bernalillo, NM 87004
505-867-3396 / Fax 505-867-3398

Contact

Randi Suzanne Malach, Director of Program Services

Population

Two Head Start programs located in a rural, multicultural county in central New Mexico. One program serves predominantly Hispanic communities; the other serves a Pueblo Indian tribe.

Initiatives

Enhances the agency's Infant and Early Childhood program by coordinating with community Head Start programs to conduct culturally appropriate parent education workshops. Staff include a professional Family Specialist and two bilingual/bicultural community liaison workers. Conduct meetings and workshops for parents and staff, offer technical assistance to Head Start staff so they can work more effectively with children and their families.

Successes

Collaborates with Head Start to provide culturally responsive family support services that meet the needs of families and staff. Both communities are striving to find a balance between the traditional and rural ways of their ancestors and contemporary society. Cultural beliefs and values greatly impact childrearing practices. Parent-community liaison workers assist in conducting workshops to ensure that material is useful and culturally appropriate. Liaison workers lead discussions in their native languages, making the setting more comfortable for many parents and extended family members to integrate their traditional beliefs with new information.

Coordinates with Head Start, local school district, and other agencies serving Hispanic communities to organize a Family Day and Health Fair. Event includes games, food, music, and free health and developmental screening for children.

Develop an interagency agreement between the agency's early intervention program, both Head Start programs, and the school district to ease the transition of 3-year-olds with developmental disabilities from early intervention into Head Start. The agency provides introductory professional development services and technical assistance to Head Start staff and families. After enrollment, Head Start and the school district provide support services to the child and additional staff development.

Kellogg Preschool Enrichment Program (KPEP)

Agency

Florida Education Fund

Contacts

Israel Tribble, Jr., President and CEO
Florida Education Fund
210 E. Kennedy Blvd., Suite 1525
Tampa, FL 33602
813-272-2772 / Fax 813-272-2784

Mary Lindsey, Executive Director
Hillsborough County Center of Excellence, Inc.
2110 North Boulevard
Tampa, FL 33602
813-229-3179 / Fax 813-221-8563

Population
Low-income African Americans and other ethnic groups in Tampa, Ft. Lauderdale, and Jacksonville, Florida.

Initiatives
Increase children's potential for school success by implementing Home Instruction Program for Preschool Youngsters (HIPPY) for children from ages 3 through 5. Parent Educators first work with family members. Parents in turn spend about 20 minutes each day doing HIPPY activities with their preschool child. Field trips, family events, workshops, and small-group discussions are included.

Improve families' self-esteem by bringing reading materials into the home and empowering parents to see themselves as teachers of, and advocates for, their children. This encourages greater parental involvement in children's education.

Increase cultural awareness by enabling families and staff to work, plan, and conduct a variety of learning and social activities together.

Successes
Family relationships are strengthened by concentrating on parents and children. Positive interactions are fostered which create feelings of success and an "I can" attitude. This process empowers parents to see themselves as their children's first teachers. KPEP families encourage others to become involved in the Initiative. Children with KPEP experience are succeeding in school and are eligible to become members of the McKnight Achievers honor society. KPEP parents volunteer in their children's schools.

Milwaukee Early Schooling Initiative

Agency
University of Wisconsin-Milwaukee

Contacts
Dominic F. Gullo, Professor of Early Childhood Education
Christine Burton-Maxwell, Assistant Professor of Early Childhood Education
Department of Curriculum and Instruction
University of Wisconsin-Milwaukee
P.O. Box 413
Milwaukee, WI 53201
414-229-5958; 4078 / Fax 414-229-5571

Martha Wheeler-Fair, Principal
Frances Starms Early Childhood Center
2616 North Garfield Avenue
Milwaukee, WI 53205
414-933-5655 / Fax 414-933-5655, ext. 5929

Joyce Taylor, Principal
Thurston Woods Campus
5966 North 35th Street
Milwaukee, WI 533209
414 536-8664

Population
Frances Starms Early Childhood Center and Thurston Woods Campus both opened as new Milwaukee Public School programs during the 1991-92 school year.

Frances Starms Early Childhood Center serves approximately 400 children from diverse ethnic (white, African American, Hmong, Native American, and Hispanic) and socioeconomic backgrounds between the ages of 3 through 6; organized into five families, each of which includes what traditionally would be two regular education classes and one special education class. Provides flexibility to use learning resources and enables full inclusion of children with special needs. Family organization promotes collaboration among staff teams of teachers, educational assistants, and specialists who integrate academic subjects including computer technology, as well as art, music, and physical education.

Thurston Woods is an ungraded primary school; 365 children between the ages of 3 and 9 attend. Mission is to develop a curriculum that promotes children's continuous learning and development across the early childhood years. Goal is to fully integrate regular and special education students.

Initiatives
Mission is to integrate the early schooling experiences of young children into comprehensive networks of support for children and their families that enhance long-term development and well-being. Accomplished through the joint efforts of public schools, community-based child care and other organizations, children's families, other formal and informal support systems, and interdisciplinary university faculty. Four interrelated goals are to

- design and implement an early childhood education model which provides for integration, continuity, and collaboration to benefit children ages birth to 8 years and their families
- design and implement a model for family-centered early childhood education
- establish collaborative linkages between public schools and community programs providing child care and other services to young children and their families
- enhance professional development opportunities for personnel within and across various early childhood settings

Successes
Modify school curriculum and instructional strategies to match characteristics and needs of enrolled children and their families. Hands-on

curriculum at Frances Starms allows students to learn through exploration and discovery. Children make choices, work cooperatively, and share thoughts and ideas, enabling them to become independent, responsible learners. Work with staff at three elementary schools to assure continuity with children's earlier experiences.

During "Child Development Days" at Thurston Woods Campus, parents bring children ages birth through 5 years for comprehensive screening. A play-based assessment follows parent interviews. Families are connected with community resources.

Establish Family Education and Support Centers and Professional Development Centers at both schools. Staff engage in professional development together and regularly exchange information and ideas.

Adopt developmentally appropriate assessment procedures at Frances Starms and redesign progress reporting system. Teachers, specialists, and parents observe each child, record behaviors, and describe the child's developmental and academic status.

Hold regular community open houses to get full community participation at Thurston Woods Campus. Individuals who may not have children in the school, such as senior citizens, are invited to visit and participate in school activities, including lunch. The number of active community volunteers increased.

My Parent(s) and Me
Washington Elementary School

Agency
Battle Creek Public Schools
Fax 616-965-9474

Contacts
Brendel Hatley, Principal
Beverly Crooks, Teacher
Washington Elementary School
450 North Washington
Battle Creek, MI 49017
616-965-9699 / Fax 616-965-9507

Initiatives
Offer Active Parenting workshop and weekly activities for parents and children. Provide Building Strong Families, a home-based parent program for urban children from birth through age 4 in collaboration with Lincoln Elementary School, 4-H, and Head Start. Offer a school-based program for children ages 3 and 4.

Successes
Increased parenting skills as measured by observations, surveys, comments, and children's preparation for school.

Increased parental attendance at school events; family pride and commitment to school and willingness to become involved.

Greater awareness about school and parenting.

Outdoor Learning Center
Post Elementary School

Agency
Battle Creek Public Schools

Contacts
Margaret Skidmore, Principal
Suzanne Cumings, Teacher
Post Elementary School
340 Cliff Street
Battle Creek, MI 49017
616-965-9687 / Fax 616-965-9507

Population
Children from birth through 5 years in a blue-collar neighborhood where many families are unemployed. The culturally diverse area includes 70% Caucasian, 20% African American, 8% Hispanic, and 2% others. About 35 to 40% are single-parent families.

Initiatives
Construct and maintain an outdoor learning center for parents and children to play, work, and learn together. Components include a garden planted by children and parents, painting easels hung on the fence, sand box, grassy area for picnics, track for riding vehicles, apple trees, log cabin playhouse, outdoor play equipment, water play, and a storage shed. Parents and young children use the facility during the school day.

Conduct monthly programs on traffic safety, how to make bird feeders, gardening, and other outdoor activity topics.

Successes
Families view the school as a safe, open, happy place. Kindergarten teachers observe that children are more comfortable on the first day of school. Children are reluctant to leave the Outdoor Learning Center.

Parents involved with the Outdoor Learning Center often become the core group of the PTA and school volunteers.

Pittsburg Pre-School Coordinating Council Co-op Project (PSCC)
National Association for the Education of Young Children / Goal One Project

Agency
Pittsburg Pre-School Coordinating Council, Inc.
1760 Chester Drive
Pittsburg, CA 94565-3920
510-439-2061 / Fax 510-432-7473

Contacts
Frances Green, Executive Director

Population
Ethnically diverse low-income families in the cities of Pittsburg, Bay Point, Antioch , and adjacent parts of Contra Costa County, California.

Initiatives
Develop a data base of community resources to increase communication and cooperation between agencies and reduce the red tape families face when they request services that will help them achieve self-sufficiency.

Develop a data base of funding sources to expand the co-op project (which offers management and training services to nonprofit agencies serving low-income minority children and families) and other community services.

Develop a close working relationship with the Contra Costa County Youth Authority, Child Protective Services, and the Pittsburg Unified School District to develop and provide delinquency prevention services and tutoring programs to the youth of the Pittsburg El Pueblo Housing Project and the city of Pittsburg. The goal is to decrease the number of at-risk students in the Pittsburg area who enter the juvenile justice system by increasing school grade averages, decreasing incidence of behavior problems in school, increasing the number of students reading at grade level, and increasing parental support for their children's academic achievement.

Successes
To date, none of the students who have attended PSCC since its inception have entered the juvenile justice system.

Eighty percent of the students in the school-age program have improved academic performance.

One local official asked to visit the program and was eventually able to generate $50,000 to support it.

Project Educational Impact (PEI) Hinks Elementary School

Agency
Alpena Public Schools

Contact
Roger Witherbee, Principal
Hinks Elementary School
7667 U.S. 23 North
Alpena, MI 49707
517-595-6226 / Fax 517-595-2562

Population
Covers 171 square miles in rural Michigan. Primarily Caucasian, with a few African American, Hispanic, and Native American families. Many families have low incomes. Ninety families, representing about two-thirds of the children who eventually enroll in kindergarten at Hinks, participate.

Initiatives
Hold a monthly meeting for all families with children from birth to age 5. Serve an informal, cafeteria-style family meal. Provide family activity and child care. In the fall, hold kick-off picnic to plant tree symbolic of growth and contributions to the school. Distribute to each family a notebook on child development resources and parenting tips. Older children receive a lap desk with crayons, markers, glue sticks, and scissors. Infants are given a blanket and set of blocks.

Arrange monthly home visits to introduce parent-child activities, play educational games, and read stories with children from birth to age 5.

Arrange for Parent Mentors who have children in the school to give newer parents the benefit of their knowledge and experience.

Successes
Attitudes in the community about the school are far more favorable. Families and children are optimistic about learning. Families make new friends, believe they are better parents, and even recruit their friends.

Families, children, and school staff get to know each other, and children are more comfortable with the school environment. The 4-year-olds and their families ride on school bus before school starts. Kindergarten children used to cry when they were dropped off at school and at lunch time in the cafeteria; now they cry when they have to leave school.

During home visits, children gain new experiences, such as carving their first pumpkin.

Parent meetings are so popular they are held two evenings each month. Parents go to great lengths to attend: A police officer arranges his lunch break at meeting time; one mother had a cesarean on Saturday, came to the parent meeting on Tuesday. Parents in all socioeconomic ranges want to be good parents and are receptive to a friendly, nonjudgmental outstretched hand.

Children who enter kindergarten after participating in PEI are "not as apprehensive, exhibiting confidence and less anxiety in dealing with adults they didn't know, self-assured and comfortable with their surroundings."

Networking within the community. School staff families get involved with the meal preparation, taking photos, making picture name tags. One parent volunteered to work with another parent who had low literacy skills; they visited the library and the school. Agencies and professionals such as a nutritionist, pediatrician, dentist, and WIC are collaborating to assure the program meets Head Start standards.

Expanded to Lincoln Elementary School and formed direct links with Head Start and Chapter I. As a result, the school, Head Start,

and Chapter I Preschool work together with children from birth through age 5.

Project First Step
National Association for the Education of Young Children / Goal One Project

Agency

Custer County Family Preservation Group, Inc.
P.O. Box 303
Broken Bow, NE 68822
308-872-2818 / Fax 308-872-6116

Contacts

Marcia Simmons, Project Coordinator
Jan McGinn, Family Resource Counselor

Population

Headquartered at Jennie M. Melham Memorial Medical Center in Broken Bow; also serves Callaway and Sargent District Hospitals. Located at the edge of the Nebraska Sandhills, a very rural, isolated expanse. Broken Bow, the largest town, has fewer than 4,000 inhabitants, mostly white. Small populations of Native Americans and Hispanics reside in the 5,500 square-mile service area that includes three counties and reaches into seven surrounding counties.

Initiatives

New Baby Program provides trained volunteers to make in-home visits to help families adjust to a new infant. Personal support and information about nutrition, immunizations, development, safety, and early learning activities are offered. Visits continue as long as the family wishes or has unmet needs.

Family Advocacy Program reduces stress for families in crisis by easing access to medical, social, or educational resources. Staff act as advocates to assist families in solving problems and working through roadblocks.

Successes

New Baby Program increases number of well-baby visits, immunizations, and health screenings. Three mothers of twins are especially grateful for home visits. Families of developmentally delayed babies were guided to appropriate services. Home visits with one mother and her infant, who was failing to thrive, brought dramatic results. The baby began to gain weight at the rate of 2 pounds a week.

Established a link with Native American families in Custer County.

None of the Project First Step families have been reported for abuse or neglect. One woman, a victim of domestic abuse, was empowered to put her life together after leaving the situation. Another domestic crisis was averted due to timely intervention by the Family Resource Counselor.

Two pregnant teens were supported in their decision to allow their babies to be adopted. Another teen mom, who chose to keep her baby, was encouraged to finish high school.

Promoting Realistic Educator-Parent Awareness for Relevant Education (P.R.E.P.A.R.E.)

Agency

Dickinson-Iron Intermediate School District
1074 Pyle Drive
Kingsford, MI 49801
906-779-2695, 2696 / Fax 906-779-2669

Contacts

Mary Brien, Superintendent
Johanna Ostwald, Administrator of Early Childhood Programs
Elizabeth Stack, Coordinator of Disability Services
Scott McClure, Principal, North and East Elementary Schools
Lee Carlson, Evaluator
Mary Jo Grippen, Parent

Population

Three elementary buildings in the Iron Mountain Public Schools in Michigan's rural Upper Peninsula serving approximately 600 children, mostly white.

Initiatives

Assist parents, teachers and administration to work together to form community-based schools. A steering committee of parents, teachers, and administrators plans, implements, and evaluates orientation activities, family nights, conferences, volunteer programs, and home visits. Strengthen family-school partnerships to provide the best learning climate for children from prep-kindergarten through second grade by offering:

Day or evening small-group, 15-hour sessions for parents and teachers to open and personalize communication. Discussion topics include team building, child guidance, school readiness, communication, philosophies, volunteer training, and goal setting to create a more effective home-school partnership.

Support for kindergarten through second-grade teachers to offer home visits to families to enable parents and teachers to work as a team to benefit the child.

Family Nights to introduce families to their elementary schools and demonstrate the value of hands-on, interactive learning.

Family Matters conferences on topics such as early reading, handling stress, child development; conferences include child care and refreshments.

Successes

Families and teachers are more comfortable

talking with each other about how best to promote individual children's learning. The number of classroom volunteers increased. Families want to stay involved in their children's education.

Children are delighted when their teachers come to their homes. Children are more successful in school and parents and teachers develop greater trust and shared expectations for children during home visits.

Family Night attendance increased dramatically. Children and families are more comfortable on the first day of school. New families feel part of the system sooner and their children get to know others before school begins.

Pumsey Circuit Breaker
J.W. Mauck Elementary School

Agency

Hillsdale Community Schools
113 E. Fayette Street
Hillsdale, MI 49242
517-437-2717; 688-4307; 523-2103; 439-5884
Fax 517-439-4194

Contacts

Martin Ryan, Principal
Joann Hess, Home School Coordinator (1992-1994)
Rickie Freeman, Home School Coordinator

Population

Small town in southeast Michigan, mostly white. A high proportion of students take part in the free and reduced-cost lunch program.

Initiatives

Build trust in school and ownership of children's education by hosting family events. Family Math and Family Reading Nights provide fun activities including a book swap run by Chapter I. Girls Night Out and Boys Night Out activities include skating, basketball, computer lab, a storyteller, and sundaes. Mauckster Mash is conducted at Halloween. Dinner with the principal is an informal winter activity, along with the all-school skate. Invitations to events are distributed to all preschools in Hillsdale, including the Hillsdale College preschool, Head Start, and Greenfield ISD.

Transition into kindergarten is eased with a bus ride, visit to the classroom, a tour of the building, and a snack in the cafeteria. Parents attend a question and answer session with principals and kindergarten teachers from all three elementary schools in Hillsdale. A community-wide celebration is held each May, complete with food, face painting, raffles, and entertainment by a fiddler, dulcimer band, and cloggers.

Children from kindergarten through 5th grade participate in a self-esteem program that encourages productive decision making. The Hillsdale College GOAL program provides tutors and mentors for students at risk.

Successes

During kindergarten registration for the 1994-95 school year, 45% of the parents chose Mauck. A father who once was leery of the school and was adamantly opposed to a PTO fundraiser now spearheads PTO fruit basket sales. In a radio interview, he stated, "At Mauck, we're always looking for ways to make it a place for the family, not just the students."

Quality Transition Program
Valley View Elementary School

Agency

Battle Creek Public Schools

Contacts

Linda Leaders, Principal
Laura Marlowe, Teacher
Valley View Elementary School
960 Avenue A
Battle Creek, MI 49017
616-965-9760 / Fax 616-965-9474

Initiatives

Offer comprehensive services.

Provide parent support meetings to engage parents in learning process.

Create an open-for-play environment that encourages parents to form partnerships with schools.

Early childhood programs that enable preschoolers to explore and use materials, ask questions, and challenge their assumptions.

Smart Start
Community Based 0-4 Transition Program
Lincoln Elementary School

Agency

Battle Creek Public Schools

Contacts

Stan Bowman, Interim Principal
Judy McReynolds, Teacher
Deborah Diget, Teacher
Lincoln Elementary School
636 W. VanBuren
Battle Creek, MI 49017
616-965-9748 / Fax 616-695-9474

Population

Families in the Lincoln School neighborhood and students with special needs drawn from the greater Battle Creek area, mostly African Americans. Many households are low-income and single parents. Children range from birth through age 8.

Initiatives

Bring warmth and enthusiasm for learning by

encouraging parents to view the school as a place for learning from birth. Provide hands-on activities, literature-enriched environments, and family homework. Help parents increase children's skills to process information, be sociable, develop small and gross motor abilities, employ sound health practices, and grow in maturity.

Parenting classes, support groups, home visits, tutorial programs, a toy lending library, and nutrition classes are provided. A resource center with a "family room" atmosphere is used by parents, children, teachers, and others. The area includes sofas, rockers, a dining table with chairs, plants, journals, and a computer.

Collaborates with Family and Children's Service, Head Start, and Calhoun County Communities in Schools.

Successes

Parents keep coming back and share their time. Family homework participation is 100%.

Many single African American fathers are involved in their children's academic development, bake cupcakes, and share their interests with children's classes.

The Staying Ahead Project
National Association for the Education of Young Children / Goal One Project

Agency

Philadelphia Parent Child Center, Inc.
25515 Germantown Avenue
Philadelphia, PA 19133
215-229-1800 / Fax 215-229-5860

Contacts

Jewel Morrissette-Ndulula, Executive Director
Shirley Stokes, Staying Ahead Project Coordinator
Wilhemina Stewart, Head Start Education Coordinator

Population

Low-income African American and Latino youth ages 10 to 14 living in North Philadelphia.

Initiatives

Supportive Youth Workers act as tutors and mentors to offer education, encourage preventive health practices, model positive parenting skills, build self-esteem, and enhance career motivation.

Successes

Establish and maintain trust among the youth, parents, Youth Workers, and school personnel.

Youth have an "I can do it" attitude and expect to be successful in the future.

Collaboration with administrators of the youth's schools reveal that the students are experiencing increased school proficiency.

Literacy games and regular exposure to the computer center enabled older children to help younger children and staff members to improve their ability to use computers.

Parents became more skilled at listening to their children.

Community support was generated by working with the Pennsylvania Department of Public Welfare, a community center, and a local university to sustain and expand outreach efforts.

Student Readiness Program
Coburn Elementary School

Agency

Battle Creek Public Schools

Contacts

Tracy Nofs, Principal
Angela Morris, Teacher
Coburn Elementary School
616-965-9730 / Fax 616-965-9474

Initiatives

Prepare children and families for school.

Integrate physical education with other play experiences in a preschool activity area.

Educate and involve parents to encourage their children's development through interaction.

Success By Six (SBS)

Agency

United Way of the Texas Gulf Coast
P.O. Box 924507
Houston, TX 77292
713-685-2812 / Fax 713-956-2868

Contacts

Lois Price, Director
Linda O'Black, Vice President of Community and Agency Support

Population

Mothers and children from before birth until age 6 living in three Houston neighborhoods. Denver Harbor is mostly Hispanic, and many residents are immigrants. About 85% of its residents are married, and average a 9th-grade education. Kashmere Gardens and Fifth Ward are primarily African American. About 95% of the mothers are single, and average an 11th-grade education. All three areas have high infant mortality rates and large numbers of low-birthweight babies; 12% of children completing kindergarten are not prepared to enter first grade.

Initiatives

Promote public awareness of optimal child growth and development prenatally through age 6.

Build families' skills in interacting with infants and young children through case management and parent education services that are family based, culturally sensitive, and coordinated. As a result, prevent child abuse and enhance children's self-esteem.

Coordinate services from health, social, and education agencies for high-risk pregnant women by referrals to physical and mental health, substance abuse, child care, education, and nutrition. Follow up to assure success.

Successes

Seventy percent of SBS participants received prenatal care during their first trimester. Average birthweight of babies born to SBS mothers is 7 pounds, 3 ounces. Reduced infant mortality rate of participants to 0%, compared to 17.6% for nonparticipants. Computerized data tracking system provides case management on all SBS participants.

Open Langston Family Life Center, a one-stop service delivery system center offering a Basic Literacy Program, Daisy Scout troop, book drive, and Bunch for Lunch program. The Langston Early Childhood Development center enrolls children ages 4 and 5, many of whom were SBS participants.

Recruit more than 110 community volunteers to work on various Initiative projects.

Collaborate with Avance-Houston, the City of Houston Parks and Recreation Department, Housing Authority, WIC Program, Houston Independent School District, First Interstate Bank, March of Dimes Foundation, Channel 2, Texas Department of Health and Human Services, Houston Police Department, Prudential Insurance Company, the American Red Cross, Texas Buddhist Association, Texas Southern University, and several other United Way agencies.

BIBLIOGRAPHY

American Academy of Pediatrics (1994). "Prime time infographic." Elk Grove Village, IL: Author.

Bredekamp, S. (Ed.). (1987). *Developmentally appropriate practice in early childhood programs serving children from birth through age 8, expanded edition*. Washington, DC: National Association for the Education of Young Children.

Bredekamp, S. & Rosegrant, T. (Eds.). (1992). *Reaching potentials: Appropriate curriculum and assessment for young children. Vol. 1.* Washington, DC: National Association for the Education of Young Children.

Carnegie Corporation of New York. (1994). *Starting points: Meeting the needs of our youngest children.* New York: Author.

Carnegie Task Force on Meeting the Needs of Young Children. (1994). *Starting points: Meeting the needs of our youngest children.* New York: Carnegie Corporation of New York.

Jachym, N., Allington, R., & Broikou, K. (1989, October). "Estimating the cost of seatwork." *The Reading Teacher*, 43(1), 30-37.

Kamii, C. (Ed.). (1990). *Achievement testing in the early grades: The games grown-ups play.* Washington, DC: National Association for the Education of Young Children.

National Association of Elementary School Principals. (1990). *Standards for quality programs for young children: Early childhood education and the elementary school principal.* Alexandria, VA: Author.

National Association of State Boards of Education. (1988). *Right from the start: The report of the NASBE Task Force on Early Childhood Education*. Alexandria, VA: Author.

National Center for Health Statistics. (1993). *Child Health USA '93*. Washington, DC: U.S Government Printing Office.

National Commission on Children. (1991). *Beyond rhetoric: A new American agenda for children and families.* Washington, DC: U.S. Government Printing Office.

National Commission on Children. (1993). *Just the facts, 1993*. Washington, DC: Author.

National Committee to Prevent Child Abuse (1994). "Some things you should know about interpersonal conflict." Chicago: Author.

National Task Force on School Readiness. (1991). *Caring communities: Supporting young children and families.* Alexandria, VA: National Association of State Boards of Education.

Peck, J.T., McCaig, G., & Sapp, M.E. (1988). *Kindergarten policies: What is best for children?* Washington, DC: National Association for the Education of Young Children.

Shepard, L. & Smith, M. (1986). "Synthesis of research on school readiness and kindergarten retention." *Educational Leadership*, 44(3) 78-86.

Stewart, A., & Gabe, T. (1991, July 30). "Head Start: Percentage of eligible children served and recent expansions." Washington, DC: Congressional Research Service, The Library of Congress.

ZERO TO THREE/National Center for Clinical Infant Programs. (1992). *Heart Start: The emotional foundations of school readiness.* Arlington, VA: Author.

Information About NAEYC

NAEYC is...

...a membership-supported organization of people committed to fostering the growth and development of children from birth through age 8. Membership is open to all who share a desire to serve and act on behalf of the needs and rights of young children.

NAEYC provides...

...educational services and resources to adults who work with and for children, including

- ***Young Children,*** *the* journal for early childhood educators
- **Books, posters, brochures,** and **videos** to expand your knowledge and commitment to young children, with topics including infants, curriculum, research, discipline, teacher education, and parent involvement
- An **Annual Conference** that brings people from all over the country to share their expertise and advocate on behalf of children and families
- **Week of the Young Child** celebrations sponsored by NAEYC Affiliate Groups across the nation to call public attention to the needs and rights of children and families
- **Insurance plans** for individuals and programs
- **Public affairs information** for knowledgeable advocacy efforts at all levels of government and through the media
- The **National Academy of Early Childhood Programs,** a voluntary accreditation system for high-quality programs for children
- The **National Institute for Early Childhood Professional Development,** providing resources and services to improve professional preparation and development of early childhood educators
- The **Information Service,** a centralized source of information sharing, distribution, and collaboration

For free information about membership, publications, or other NAEYC services...

- call NAEYC at 202-232-8777 or 800-424-2460
- or write to NAEYC, 1509 16th St., N.W., Washington, DC 20036-1426.